The Shakesp

THE SHAKESPEARE HANDBOOKS

Series Editor: John Russell Brown

PUBLISHED

John Russell Brown	*Hamlet*
John Russell Brown	*Macbeth*
Paul Edmondson	*Twelfth Night*
Bridget Escolme	*Antony and Cleopatra*
Kevin Ewert	*Henry V*
Trevor R. Griffiths	*The Tempest*
Stuart Hampton-Reeves	*Measure for Measure*
Margaret Jane Kidnie	*The Taming of the Shrew*
Christopher McCullough	*The Merchant of Venice*
Paul Prescott	*Richard III*
Lesley Wade Soule	*As You Like It*

FORTHCOMING

Roger Apfelbaum	*Much Ado About Nothing*
John Russell Brown	*King Lear*
David Carnegie	*Julius Caesar*
James Loehlin	*Henry IV: Parts 1 and 2*
Edward L. Rocklin	*Romeo and Juliet*
Martin White	*A Midsummer Night's Dream*

The Shakespeare Handbooks

Measure for Measure

Stuart Hampton-Reeves

First published 2007 by
PALGRAVE MACMILLAN
Houndmills, Basingstoke, Hampshire RG21 6XS and
175 Fifth Avenue, New York, N.Y. 10010
Companies and representatives throughout the world

PALGRAVE MACMILLAN is the global academic imprint of the Palgrave Macmillan division of St. Martin's Press, LLC and of Palgrave Macmillan Ltd. Macmillan® is a registered trademark in the United States, United Kingdom and other countries. Palgrave is a registered trademark in the European Union and other countries.

ISBN-13: 978–1–4039–4416–0 hardback
ISBN 10: 1–4039–4416–4   hardback
ISBN-13: 978–1–4039–4417–7 paperback
ISBN 10: 1–4039–4417–2   paperback

This book is printed on paper suitable for recycling and made from fully managed and sustained forest sources.

A catalogue record for this book is available from the British Library.

A catalog record for this book is available from the Library of Congress.

10   9   8   7   6   5   4   3   2   1
16   15   14   13   12   11   10   09   08   07

Printed in China

Contents

General Editor's Preface

The Shakespeare Handbooks provide an innovative way of studying the theatrical life of the plays. The commentaries, which are their core feature, enable a reader to envisage the words of a text unfurling in performance, involving actions and meanings not readily perceived except in rehearsal or performance. The aim is to present the plays in the environment for which they were written and to offer an experience as close as possible to an audience's progressive experience of a production.

While each book has the same range of contents, their authors have been encouraged to shape them according to their own critical and scholarly understanding and their first-hand experience of theatre practice. The various chapters are designed to complement the commentaries: the cultural context of each play is presented together with quotations from original sources; the authority of its text or texts is considered with what is known of the earliest performances; key performances and productions of its subsequent stage history are both described and compared. The aim in all this has been to help readers to develop their own informed and imaginative view of a play in ways that supplement the provision of standard editions and are more user-friendly than detailed stage histories or collections of criticism from diverse sources.

Further volumes are in preparation so that, within a few years, the Shakespeare Handbooks will be available for all the plays that are frequently studied and performed.

John Russell Brown

Preface

In writing this book, I benefited a great deal from being given the opportunity to observe and work with David Pearce and his acting class at the University of Central Lancashire. Many of the insights generated by discussions and exercises developed by the class have directly shaped my approach to the play. In writing this book, I've aimed to identify some of the problems that confront actors and directors when they work with the text. As will quickly become apparent, there is no correct way to perform the play. On the contrary, I have tried as much as possible to draw attention to questions which the text raises but does not answer. It is through grappling with the play's many gaps and silences that theatrical *and* critical interpretations are formed. This is more evident in the open, experimental space of studio rehearsal, so I am indebted to David and his class for giving me the opportunity to explore these performance cruxes through creative performance workshops first before daring to write about them. I should also like to thank Debbie Williams and John Russell Brown for their comments and support. I hope this book will be useful to actors and readers as well as actors who like to read and readers who like to act, or like to imagine themselves acting.

1 The Text and Early Performances

Measure for Measure has a small cast but it deals with big themes. The play includes some of Shakespeare's most powerful lines about the terror of death, and few of his plays are more cynical about the business of love. As it probes political corruption and sexual deviance, the play asks angry, insistent questions. Yet the play offers few answers. Some find this troubling and consequently, in modern times, the play has been burdened with the wholly unattractive and inappropriate label 'problem play'. *Hamlet* is clearly a tragedy, there is no question that *As You Like It* is a comedy, but poor, ugly *Measure for Measure* is treated with puzzlement. There is no such genre as a 'problem play'. It is we who have the problem.

This may be because *Measure for Measure* is not a particularly 'readerly' play. We do not expect this from Shakespeare, who is usually attentive to both readers and public audiences. To just glance over the text reveals an unpromising prospect for performance. Long speeches follow long speeches, scenes between two characters stretch for pages with much argument but little action. At times, the text seems stuck in complicated disputations of legal niceties and moral dilemmas which seem to be of their time, not ours. However, to merely read *Measure for Measure* is to misread it, for its real drama lies in what is not said. Few other plays by Shakespeare depend so much on unspoken thoughts and passions driving the action. *Measure for Measure* comes alive in its subtext, in unspoken thoughts and feelings. As the text is worked on in the studio, its secrets and its silences become ever more important.

First performances

Measure for Measure was, like all of Shakespeare's plays, written for performance, but the circumstances of its performance was highly unusual. The play is tightly bound up with the cultural politics of 1604, the year when James I formally took his throne (having inherited it the previous year from his cousin Elizabeth). James was already King of Scotland, so his political views were well known, and many are reflected in *Measure for Measure*. He was certainly in the audience when the King's Men performed it at court during the Christmas festivities of 1604. However, the play was not written to simply flatter one man. It had been in the King's Men's repertoire for some months and was probably first staged in April that year at the Globe playhouse in Southwark.

Measure for Measure balances these different audience positions without ever resolving them. The play moves between the two different worlds of court and city, between the high culture of dukes and the low culture of prostitutes, pimps and thieves. In both worlds, we see characters fretting about the nature of authority and suffering when authority is misapplied. It is no coincidence that Shakespeare and his company also moved between those worlds, playing in the city's 'red light' district most of the time but also playing at court when summoned. Those in the audience at the court were invited to see in the play's representation of justice a mirror for themselves. However, Shakespeare's city audiences were much more sceptical about authority. They would have found common cause with the play's rogues and rakes, for whom the sudden imposition of strict law is a nuisance and, in one case, nearly a tragedy.

The two principal theatrical spaces for which Shakespeare wrote *Measure for Measure* were strikingly different. At court, the actors played at one end of a hall. If in attendance, the King was the most important participant, to some extent the main audience, and in many respects a more important spectacle than the show itself. The actor–audience dynamic closely resembled the ritual relationship between monarch and subject: the actors faced their audience and projected to them. The theatrical dynamics at the Globe were quite different. Plays were performed in the open air. Through a simple payment system, audiences were socially stratified, with the more wealthy patrons on sheltered benches and those who either couldn't or wouldn't pay more than a penny standing in the open area in front of the stage, the pit. A large thrust stage brought the action right into the audience and an actor could address their audience from three different sides, encouraging an intimacy between actors and audiences quite different to that at court. This was more than a feigned intimacy: there were usually only sixteen or so players in the King's Men and most of them specialized in playing certain kinds of roles. Audiences knew the players well and knew their other roles. Richard Burbage was Shakespeare's lead actor and would most likely have played the Duke, but he was also this audience's Hamlet, their Henry V, and so on. Equally, as the company put on shows daily and probably played a very varied programme (we know from surviving account books that the rival Rose playhouse put on a different play virtually every day), the actors probably knew the audience, or certain characters in the audience, as well. The players had only themselves, their costumes and a few props to create their Vienna. No women were allowed to act, so all women's parts would have been played by adolescent boys (Mistress Overdone is still often played by a man).

Because these spaces and audiences were so familiar, *Measure for Measure* was able to address them directly. Shakespeare had good reason to be strategic. The year 1604 was an anxious one because it was the first proper year of a new regime. *Measure for Measure* is, on one level, a play about succession management. For at least a decade before this, Shakespeare and his contemporaries had worried endlessly about what would happen to the country (and to their positions, their wealth, and so on) when the childless Elizabeth died, an event which could have come at any time. So destabilizing was this anxiety that Elizabeth outlawed any talk of it. Yet people always talk when a new regime is coming and the literature of these years is thick with the horrors of civil war. Shakespeare himself wrote seven plays about English civil war in almost as many years. A violent political struggle was a real possibility, especially in a country still stalked by the spectre of religious radicalism and still looked upon as a rogue state ripe for invasion by its neighbours. In the event, James's accession went very smoothly and his formal entry into London through its city gates in 1604 was a memorable event. Shakespeare was part of the spectacle and he recalled it in the closing scene of *Measure for Measure*, which is based around the triumphant return of the Duke of Vienna through its city gates. Nevertheless, doubts and worries lingered. *Measure for Measure* is a product of that moment and seems to be a different play depending on which audience one imagines watching it. It is a strong affirmation of the importance of good governance for a court audience, and a cynical satire about the inconvenience of over-zealous authoritarianism for a city audience. Both plays exist in the same text, measure for measure.

The text

Measure for Measure was first published in 1623, nearly twenty years after it was written, when it was included as one of the comedies in Shakespeare's first complete works, edited by two of his fellow King's Men, John Hemminges and William Condell. The actual text was prepared by a scribe called Ralph Crane, who appears to have introduced changes to the text when he thought fit. The text shows signs of being edited after performances, perhaps to accommodate different circumstances, perhaps because a scene did not work as well on the stage as it did on the page. This leads to some curious plot-holes. In Act I, scene ii, one character, Mistress Overdone, rushes to tell her clients that their friend Claudio has been taken to prison. Later in the scene, she seems to not yet know about his arrest. However, these are relatively minor inconsistencies which can easily be straightened out in the rehearsal room.

It's a truism to say that a play is 'written for performance'. The text that we have of *Measure for Measure* was prepared long after Shakespeare and his company had put the play into performance. Its performance context shapes its text. For example, in addressing the play's protean ability to mean different things to court and city audiences, Leah Marcus wonders if *Measure for Measure* is actually two plays or 'double written' (Marcus, p. 164). In similar terms, many critics have attempted to account for the way that the city and the court plays work together or against each other in the text. Understanding the conditions of the play's first performances in 1604 shed much light on why the play is 'double written'. Shakespeare had two audiences to write for in a climate where the nature of authority, following the accession of a new king and the founding of a new royal dynasty, was very much at the forefront of people's minds.

The play's twin performance contexts of court and city are reflected in the text. The play is set in Vienna which, after years of lax rule, has become a haven for promiscuous young men who want to dodge marriage and cavort with prostitutes. At court, the Duke, appalled by the state of the city, decides to disguise himself as a friar and explore it for himself. Meanwhile, he leaves in charge a straight-laced bureaucrat, Angelo, who he knows will ruthlessly enforce Vienna's long-abused laws against illicit sex. The court and the city quickly become entangled when Angelo sentences to death one young rake, Claudio, for getting his fiancée pregnant. For Angelo, the distinction between court and city is an absolute one but he discovers his own hypocrisy when Claudio's sister, Isabella, pleads with him for her brother's life. Angelo becomes infatuated with Isabella and proposes a bargain: if she sleeps with him, he will release Claudio. The story of the corrupt judge was already an old one when Shakespeare wrote it. His innovation was to add to the story the disguised Duke (Shakespeare may well have had in mind the rumour that James I liked to go incognito about the city) who lingers around the prison and discovers Angelo's crime. The play then pits the Duke's governance against Angelo's. The Duke tries to trick the trickster by substituting Isabella for Marianna, a woman to whom Angelo was once betrothed but who he cruelly abandoned. In this way, justice appears to be done, because it is no crime for Angelo to sleep with a woman who is nearly his wife. Court and city come together in the play's dramatic final scene, when the Duke pretends to return to Vienna and discovers Angelo's crime, and eventually reveals himself to be the Friar who has helped Isabella. However, this ending does not simply celebrate the restoration of order. True, Angelo is exposed, but he and Marianna are punished with a loveless marriage, and Vienna seems to remain as bad a place as it was at the start.

The text is full of gaps and silences. The most famous comes at the end. Almost as an afterthought, the Duke proposes to marry Isabella, a young woman who, at the start of the play, was training to be a nun. Until this point, there has been no romance between them. Isabella is apparently speechless. That is to say, she has no lines, but an actress still has to speak, even if it is silently. Isabella cannot just stand there as if nothing has happened; the Duke's proposal is a startling and unexpected twist that demands some kind of response. The text is full of such lacunae. The only arguably happy marriage appears to be that of Claudio and Juliet. However, the text gives little indication about how deeply their love runs. Their marriage is mentioned briefly and as a punishment, as the Duke says: 'She,' [burying Juliet in a dismissive pronoun] 'that you wronged, look you restore' (V.i.517). That is all the text gives us. Productions often compensate for this by staging a joyful reunion between Claudio and Juliet, who enters carrying her illegitimate baby (which would have been far too shameful a thing for an early modern Juliet to do) and stands in Claudio's arms, together the very image of a young, happy family. It is surprising how little the text provides to support this reading. No baby is mentioned; they have no lines (Claudio is silent for the whole scene, as is Juliet) and no stage actions. Very little is said about their love in the preceding text. Claudio mentions Juliet once in the whole play and that is when he is defending himself against his arrest. He insists to his friend Lucio that Juliet is 'fast my wife', that they were only hiding their love because Juliet did not have the money for a dowry and that her pregnancy was an unhappy accident. Claudio's language is not love poetry and what he says smacks more of special pleading (I was going to marry her, honestly) than sincere emotion. Claudio and Juliet are hardly Romeo and Juliet. In fact, Claudio does not speak to Juliet in the whole play – not once.

Isabella is not alone in her silence, then. In fact speech and silence is one of the play's major themes and is linked to authority in the opening, when the Duke worries that anatomizing the work of government would affect 'speech and discourse' (I.i.4) and shortly afterwards says to his favourite Angelo, 'I do bend my speech' (40), before exhorting him to 'live in thy tongue' (45). He makes Angelo his Deputy and then leaves. His other adviser, Escalus, asks Angelo permission 'to have free speech' with him (i.e. speak freely) (77). Speech is not free in Vienna and, despite the Duke's opening lines, speech is already twisted, as is evidenced by the convoluted sexual puns (now inaccessible to most modern audiences) that dart back and forth between the wit Lucio and two soldiers he enters with in Act I, scene ii.

Speech is also linked to resistance. Claudio asks Lucio to 'implore' Isabella 'in my voice' and Lucio chides Isabella for having too 'tame' a tongue. Readying for the Duke's formal return, Isabella is loath 'to speak so indirectly' (IV.vi.1) as the Duke (as the Friar) has persuaded her to do but, when she faces the Duke and the court, she insists, 'I must speak' (30) and 'Most strange, but yet most truly will I speak' (37) which the Duke, playing a part, dismisses as mad speech: 'She speaks this in th'infirmity of sense' (48). Isabella, who began the play discussing the nunnery's strict rules about speaking to men and has to answer the door because she is the only one there who *can* speak to Lucio (having not yet taken her vows), ends by speaking for Marianna (now Angelo's wife) and pleading for Angelo's life. However, it is not Isabella's speech but her silence that Claudio and Marianna want her for. Claudio tells Lucio that Isabella has a 'prone and speechless dialect' (I.ii.164); Marianna never asks Isabella to speak for Angelo but merely to kneel and 'hold up your hands' but 'say nothing; I'll speak all' (V.i.431–2). Both want Isabella to be still and silent, but defying both and her 'destined livery' at the nunnery, Isabella speaks. Even the Duke does not want a talking Isabella for, as he leads her offstage, he asks her, 'if you'll a willing ear incline', to listen to him (V.i.28). Isabella's silence is not, then, an authorial oversight; she is deliberately silenced by the Duke who wants her only to listen to him. Still and speechless, or holding her hands up in silence, or inclining her ear to listen but not speak, Isabella is disempowered through silence. Ironically, the only person who wants her speech is Angelo who, seduced by her voice, says to himself, 'I desire to hear her speak again' (I.ii.182). In II.iv, Angelo's chat-up line is 'I do arrest your words' (135), to which Isabella begs 'I have no tongue but one . . . Let me entreat you speak the former language' (140–1). The doubleness of language and the important role of speech in authority, whether speech is a way of policing people (ironic then that the play's only policeman, Elbow, cannot speak properly but inverts everything), reflect the deeply ingrained duality of the play.

A note on the text

The edition of *Measure for Measure* used throughout this book is the New Cambridge Shakespeare edited by Brian Gibbons, which is among the best of the modern editions and was revised for a second edition in 2006. It is also a very practical text for the rehearsal room, as its footnotes do not take up much of the page.

One of the distinctive features of Gibbons's edition is his verse-lining of half-lines. For example, Gibbons classes the following two lines as one:

ISABELLA   Must he needs die?
ANGELO   Maiden, no remedy. (II.ii.49)

Although there are two lines to be spoken, together they comprise one line of iambic pentameter. This is a helpful way to signal how artfully Shakespeare links certain characters and ideas in verse, and I have retained Gibbons's verse lining for my scene notes.

In principle, this book can be used with most editions of the play which, as discussed above, do not vary significantly because there is only one authoritative text for editors to work from. Nevertheless, there are going to be minor discrepancies from edition to edition, and a group of students or actors should at least endeavour to all buy the same edition to avoid confusion.

2 Commentary

Act I, scene i

The play begins with a certain amount of confusion. The Duke is inexplicably anxious, his speech unnecessarily convoluted, his intentions unclear to his subordinates who are stunned by his unannounced abrogation of power. Although some of the speeches are long, they should be delivered hastily. The Duke is being abstruse and unpredictable. As soon as he has taken Escalus into his confidence, he immediately makes Angelo his Deputy. For Angelo and Escalus and perhaps for the audience as well, the Duke's behaviour is utterly baffling. Angelo especially seems uncomfortable with his promotion.

1–2 With one word, the Duke defines his relationship with Escalus: he is familiar and is confident that merely saying Escalus' name is sufficient to command the old man's attention. With two words spoken in response, Escalus signals his subservience. As the audience do not know who either of these men are, this little exchange is very important in establishing the political relationship between them. How the lines are delivered then becomes a crucial question, as it is very easy to load both lines with irony, uncertainty, tetchiness, even affection.

The text does not tell us why the Duke needs to call Escalus. Presumably they do not enter together, or if they do it is with a crowd of attendants. The Duke could be taking Escalus aside, in which case l. 2 might even register a note of surprise at his attention; the Duke could publicly summon Escalus to his side, which makes l. 1

9

commanding and confident. Alternatively, the Duke could be in a throne, Escalus standing at his side waiting to be summoned. A pause can be introduced for comic effect; for a more serious reading, the Duke could speak in a dark, commanding way, Escalus responding quickly and with humility.

5–23   The Duke's first long speech is awkward and curiously self-depreciating. Escalus may well be as baffled as the audience by the Duke's tortuous language. There are many different clauses in the passage which suggest the Duke's disordered mind. For example, ll. 6–9 contains nine clauses; in l. 8, the Duke basically says nothing in ten words. The Duke is noticeably less authoritarian with Escalus than he is with Angelo later. The commission that the Duke gives to Escalus is likely to be a scroll or letter with a royal seal given to Escalus during this speech.

The Duke calls to an attendant to bring Angelo in and then turns back to Escalus, to whom he looks for reassurance that he has picked the right man. A couple of times he asks Escalus for his opinion. The Duke's uncertainties will vanish when Angelo enters; Escalus responds with a classic 'yes-man' answer which clearly does not settle the Duke, who does not reply but instead spots Angelo entering.

24–7   When Angelo enters the stage, the Duke does not greet him at first even though he signals to Escalus that Angelo is approaching (l. 24). Rather, it is Angelo who speaks first, his two lines (ll. 25–6) acknowledging the Duke's authority.

That Angelo speaks first seems significant, as Escalus earlier waited to be called. The Duke could be feigning a certain amount of indifference to his Deputy, in which case this is the first time we can see him plainly playing a role. L. 24 tells us that the Duke is keenly interested to know that Angelo has arrived, so it is not through ignorance or indifference that he does not first speak to him. Rather, the Duke is pretending to be aloof, forcing Angelo to be patient and deferential. Such strategies suggest that, from the outset, the Duke has it in mind to test his favourite.

Alternatively, Angelo could speak his lines before the Duke has an opportunity to say anything to him. In this reading, Angelo is so eager to know what it is the Duke wants (suspecting that it is to his advantage) that he blurts out a greeting without following proper decorum. This Angelo is greedy and ambitious. L. 26 will be echoed later by Isabella (II.iv.31), when the conjunction of the words 'come' and 'pleasure' will be taken by Angelo as a good sign that she will be easily bedded. The Duke's next line, timed right with a slight pause following it, should be funny. By saying his name, the Duke stops his eager Deputy for a moment and forces him to listen to a long speech which takes some time (perhaps deliberately) to come to a point.

27–47   The Duke's manner changes as he launches into a speech full of observations, parables and instructions. Like many of his lengthier speeches, it is full of pompous waffle and wanders around the point. The Duke enjoys pontificating, but his audiences must often have been either confused or bored by his little sermons. This one is especially puzzling, as the Duke rather tortuously explains to Angelo why he must give himself up for public service, even though he seems to need little persuading.

The speech can be divided into two parts.

In ll. 27–40, the Duke coaxes Angelo with attractive arguments. He flatters him (l. 28) and insists that he would be selfish not to share his talents (l. 31). This is clearly a ruse and Angelo will already be curious to know why the Duke is taking so long to get to the point. Flattery from a Duke usually comes at a price.

From the second half of l. 40, the Duke seems to suddenly become impatient with persuasion and instead rushes to his point. This part of the speech is more hurried and urgent. The Duke signals that he has arrived at his point by his half-line at l. 42, which should be strong and serious.

He reminds Angelo of Escalus' position – both 'first in question' and secondary – and gives Angelo his commission, which again will be a physical object, a scroll or a letter. In this, the Duke acts much more pompously than he did before when he gave Escalus his commission, and the Duke has dropped the persuasive tone of the first part of his speech. L. 47, another half-line, is as clear a statement as the Duke has yet made and it is an order, not a request.

47–50 Shakespeare uses a half-line technique for the first here which he will later use to great effect in the two scenes in which Angelo interviews Isabella. The Duke ends his speech with a line of just five beats; Angelo's next few words complete the line, so metrically linking his words with the Duke's. This creates a sing-song effect not unlike the 'call-and-response' technique in jazz improvization. As with Angelo and Isabella's scenes in Act II, there is a certain amount of game-playing at work, the Duke playing one side, Angelo the other. In this case, the Duke and Angelo are moving towards the same end. This technique is continued until l. 60.

Angelo's speech is deferential and similar in tone to Escalus' earlier lines 22–4. Angelo may be showing some false modesty here, but he could be genuinely nervous about taking on the responsibilities of leadership. His reply is the first so far to match the Duke's speech for metaphorical flourish and shows a certain amount of confidence. Whatever he might say, Angelo clearly feels equal to the task of running the country.

50–75 The Duke has no patience for Angelo's insincere self-doubts: instead of offering tender encouragement and paternal wisdom, he is brisk (l. 50) and now seems anxious to leave the stage as fast as possible. Angelo's attempt to intervene (ll. 60–1) only makes the Duke keener to escape. He issues a hasty order and then, strangely, seems to feign shyness (ll. 67–8). The Duke's language is characterized by speed: 'haste' (said twice), 'quick', 'away'. The Duke takes Angelo's hands, refers to the commissions he has given his deputies, and says 'fare you well' three times. The Duke is in a hurry and he leaves anxiously, without ceremony, not like a Duke but like a businessman late for his train. Angelo and Escalus struggle to maintain some formality, but the Duke is quick to leave the stage.

76–84 The deputies are left bewildered by the Duke's strange behaviour and uncertain about their responsibilities. If Escalus previously was happy to agree with all of the Duke's propositions, now alone with Angelo he quickly admits that he has much on his mind. When he asks Angelo politely for 'free speech', Escalus hints that his words up until now have not been free at all. Escalus' position is unclear, and he ponders what powers and responsibilities his authority will actually give him (ll. 79–80).

Angelo is likewise confused, but he quickly adapts to his new role. He takes Escalus aside for a discussion in private, just as the Duke did at the start of the scene. Following the Duke's abrupt departure, structures of power and deference have been reconstituted, albeit vaguely.

Act I, scene ii

With the change in setting from the court to the street, the two principal spheres of action are now established. This scene is a long one which brings together several different episodes (some productions split them up so that Lucio's verbal joust with the Gentlemen, Mistress Overdone's reflections on the state of the trade and Claudio's arrest occur in different places about the city). Visually, Lucio's entrance mirrors that of the Duke's, as he is also flanked by two companions. Lucio's banter with the two Gentlemen (actually, they are two soldiers) is difficult for modern audiences to follow but the basic thrust of the exchange can be made clearer if the actors make plain the dialogue's ribald subtext. So fast-moving is this exchange that its meaning is easily lost in performance, but its core dramatic idea is simple: Lucio is playing a game of wits with two soldiers. The second soldier is quickly defeated when Lucio and the First Gentleman gang up on him, and for a moment the First Gentleman thinks he has beaten Lucio, but Lucio is the better wit and manipulates the conversation from the start. He traps the First Gentleman with a quip and wins the battle of wits. Although the Gentlemen do not appear again in the play, they help to establish Lucio and the city's underworld, and creative directors can find other ways to use the soldiers later in the production (as prison guards, for example).

Because the scene begins in the middle of the conversation, it is tempting to overlap its start with the end of the previous scene. However, there is a jump in time which might be better signalled by a pause between scenes: this scene takes place a few days after the previous one, the Duke is away (as Lucio tells us in his first line) and Angelo has already started to enforce his rule (as we learn later).

1–8 Lucio is a streetwise 'wide boy' and an armchair commentator; the two Gentlemen are, we learn, soldiers itching for war and are in town, apparently for some 'r-and-r'. They enter together and they are already deep into a game of wits. Lucio is winding the soldiers up by suggesting that there might soon be peace if the Duke's negotiations with Hungary succeed (l. 1). Lucio is no expert on politics (a point which will later become clear); he is simply needling the soldiers, who will be out of a job if the war ends.

The First Gentleman bristles and protests that he does not want peace at all. His companion readily agrees (ll. 3–5). They both use the language of religious ceremony to make a secular point. The First Gentleman's reference to heaven (l. 3) is echoed by the Second's 'Amen' (l. 5).

Lucio picks up on the Gentlemen's comic piety (praying for war) with the clever image of a pirate who diligently observes all of the Ten Commandments except 'thou shalt not steal' (ll. 6–8). By this, Lucio mocks the Second Gentleman's 'Amen' and goads his companions further, both of whom fall into the trap of debating the ethics of being a soldier.

9–19 The First Gentleman jokingly defends Lucio's imagined sanctimonious pirate and says that, by the same token, soldiers do not like to hear prayers for peace when saying grace (ll. 11–14). The Second Gentleman appears to take his colleague's joke literally and upbraids him for what he sees as a slur on their profession (l. 15). His error is a gift to Lucio, who immediately starts to wind the soldier up (l. 16). The Second Gentleman falls into the trap (l. 17) – he's only heard grace said a dozen times. In the next few lines, Lucio and the First Gentleman gang up on the Second for this admission.

20–3 Tiring of baiting the Second Gentleman, at l. 20 Lucio switches to mocking the First. Returning to the theme of grace, Lucio calls his companion a villain without any grace (l. 22), to which the First Gentleman scoffs that in that case there is little difference between himself and Lucio (l. 23). The First Gentleman is a sharper wit than the Second and thinks himself more than a match for Lucio.

24–8   This is a difficult passage for modern audiences and may need gestures to make its sexual meaning obvious. The 'list' of a cloth is the plain edge that is often cut when the cloth is being prepared (Gibbons, p. 85). If Lucio and the First Gentleman are cut from the same cloth, Lucio jokes, then the First Gentleman is the discarded 'list' and Lucio is the quality velvet. The First Gentleman hits back by calling Lucio a pretentious 'three-piled' French velvet: he would rather be plain and honest (and English) than the pompous, vain and over-the-top 'three-piled' velvet.

29–34   The First Gentleman thinks he has the upper hand (l. 29). However, Lucio interprets 'feelingly' as 'painfully' and mocks the First Gentleman for having mouth ulcers, which is why he then refuses to drink from the same glass (to avoid catching the ulcers). The First Gentleman admits his defeat; the Second Gentleman, sensing that he is no longer a target, adds a little dig of his own, implying that the First Gentleman is infected with venereal disease.

35–45   Although Lucio spots Mistress Overdone offstage at l. 35, she says nothing for nearly fifteen lines. Either she takes some time to cross the stage (difficult to do on the relatively shallow stage at the Globe) or, more likely, the three men intend that she should hear their teasing banter about the diseases they have caught at her brothel. Having previously competed with each other, the three men now gang together. They continue as if still playing a game with each other, but their banter is really directed at Overdone.

  When the First Gentleman uses Lucio's admission that he has bought many diseases (i.e. contracted venereal disease from prostitutes) to try and win back some ground (ll. 42–3), Lucio proves again that he is the better wit by pointing out that 'sound' things are hollow (ll. 44–5).

46–7   The First Gentleman escapes by addressing Overdone, who the men have, until now, been pretending to ignore. He is familiar with her and teases her with an insult about her body. He may mean his comment to be an affectionate dig, but it is really a vicious insult (l. 46).

48–58   Overdone is not easily cowed. Besides, she has news, which she uses to puncture the men's jocular mood. She begins with a boast that someone has been arrested more worthy than any of them, which provokes the Second Gentleman to ask petulantly who that might be (ll. 50–1). When she says Claudio's name, things become more serious. The First Gentleman is shocked (l. 53).

Overdone, a natural gossip, is more interested in telling them the gory details (ll. 54–6) – she even seems to allude to castration (her reference to Claudio's head is a *double entendre*). However, Lucio is no longer in the mood for such jokes and he presses her to tell him the full story (ll. 57–8).

59–66   Overdone eagerly tells them about Juliet's pregnancy (ll. 59–60). The three men are now worried; there is little room for humour in l. 61, although there is an ambiguity about whether Lucio is responding to the news of Claudio's capture or Juliet's condition. The following lines clearly signal how seriously he takes the news.

Ll. 61–2 are addressed to the two Gentlemen. All three realize that Overdone is not joking and the two Gentlemen quickly connect Claudio's arrest with Angelo's proclamation, which we now learn they were discussing earlier. Lucio is concerned about Claudio; the two Gentlemen are thinking about themselves. If Claudio can be arrested for *that*, then none of them are safe. They leave the stage quickly, perhaps through the same door through which Overdone entered, as we know that she has just seen Claudio being taken to prison. The men ignore Overdone. This sets up the tragicomic pathos for her short soliloquy.

67–9   When Mistress Overdone briefly takes centre stage, it is the first time in the play that the stage has been almost empty. Her lines appear to be addressed to the audience as a complaint: because of war, disease, poverty and punters being hanged, I have no business for my brothels. However, these lines could just as successfully be played as a comment to herself, looking after the men who have gone to find out more about Claudio. A brothel-keeper's complaint is likely to raise a laugh but the line sets a bleak urban context.

70–97 This scene has often puzzled scholars because Mistress Overdone, having told Lucio about Claudio's arrest, now seems not to know anything about it. This might be evidence of textual corruption although some (such as Bawcutt, pp. 72–3) have ventured other explanations, e.g. that Overdone is 'dim-witted' and slow to realize that Pompey's 'yonder man' is Claudio. From a theatrical point of view, it is helpful to the audience to hear Claudio's story again.

Another is to develop the point that Overdone does not yet know about the proclamation – this is strongly implied in her address to the audience and confirmed later in this exchange. Her lines can then be read as expressions of amazement by someone who knows what has happened (Claudio has been arrested, etc.), but not why. Pompey's extravagant replies, which do not answer her questions, can then be seen as evasions. L. 72 can be read with a worldly-wise 'well' and then 'what has he done' as a rhetorical question, i.e. 'what has he done that is so serious?' (implying that she knows his crime and thinks it trivial); l. 74 as 'but what's so wrong about premarital sex?' and l. 76 with a dismissive 'what' followed by a sarcastic delivery of the rest of the line. That Pompey realizes from all this that Overdone does not know about the proclamation and does not know about Angelo's crackdown on sex laws supports this reading.

The rest of this section is straightforward, although audiences might need some visual clues to understand that Overdone is a prostitute, Pompey her pimp. Overdone is worried about her future under this new, censorious regime (l. 88). Pompey comforts her, mixing tender concern with a business proposition (l. 91).

Overdone spots Claudio entering and Pompey helpfully names the principals for us, suggesting some overlap between their exit and Claudio's entrance. However, as Overdone says 'let's withdraw' (ll. 94–5), there is justification for keeping Overdone and Pompey at the rear or side of the stage, continuing to watch the rest of the scene.

98–105 After much heralding, we finally get to see Claudio. He is being publicly paraded as part of his punishment and as a warning to others (l. 98). That he is a prisoner will need to be clearly signalled: simple manacles are an obvious way of showing this. However, actors might find it useful to explore different ways in which Claudio's captivity can be played (and resisted) through gesture and body posture. Claudio's public humiliation is meant as a demonstration of Angelo's new crackdown.

Ll. 98–9 can be played as either a melancholy plea that shows what a sensitive soul the young rake is or as an angry protest. We will later learn that Claudio is not cut out for heroic tragedy, so these lines might be treated as a bit of a front designed to impress his friends. In truth, Claudio is very much in charge of the dialogue at this point, despite being physically restrained.

The Provost is clearly uncomfortable with this display and tries to absolve himself (l. 100) by blaming Angelo instead. Claudio's next lines are ripe with mannered pathos and are perhaps meant to be heard by everyone onstage. He does not really believe that his punishment is 'just', but he might believe that Angelo is merely testing him.

Shakespeare does not tell us anything about Juliet, but she is an important non-speaking part since it is her pregnancy which is at issue. Some companies have made her pregnancy very obvious, though this tends to raise a sense of absurdity about the scene; others bring out the pathos. Why is she silent? Does she choose not to speak, does she try to speak and is prevented, is she following the procession or is she a part of the humiliation ritual? There are more silent characters. The soldiers play no role in this dialogue and could be cut; if Overdone and Pompey are still onstage, they also say nothing, but watch.

106–16 Lucio interrupts Claudio's sombre reflections on authority and justice (l. 106).

Claudio's character is clearly established in the following lines. To begin with he is melancholy and resigned, reflecting philosophically on authority, justice and death. He is familiar; he calls Lucio 'my Lucio', implying an affection between them which is not seen again in the play (l. 107). He is eager (perhaps too eager) to sound repentant and even seems to accept the inevitability of his death (l. 112) for having indulged too much liberty.

Lucio mocks his friend for speaking like this. He boasts that he could not speak so eloquently if he were arrested, but even if he could, he would prefer to stay free (ll. 113–15). He is not there to listen to Claudio repent his sins; he wants to know what Claudio has done.

117–25   At first, Claudio carries on playing the role of the contrite sinner by refusing to say directly what it is he has done and even making Lucio think his crime is as serious as murder (l. 121). Lucio thinks carefully about what kind of man his friend is and, looking past Claudio's melancholic demeanour, rightly guesses that it is not murder but a sex crime that has led to his arrest (l. 120). 'Lechery' might be said with a glance at Juliet, whose presence (and pregnancy, if visible) confirms Overdone's gossip (l. 120).

Even now, Claudio appears to continue acting in a self-pitying, mock-heroic fashion, but the Provost insists that they leave (l. 122). Claudio's manner quickly changes: he has business to do, he does not really want to be executed and Lucio might be able to help him. He is now brisk, tells the Provost to wait (a very confident thing for a condemned man to do) and takes Lucio to one side for a brief word.

Once again, we have a character, this time Lucio, appearing not to know Claudio's crime despite being told earlier in the scene. Theatrically, the story is reinforced; in terms of character logic, perhaps the best explanation is that Lucio does not trust Mistress Overdone and can't believe that Claudio would be arrested and paraded thus simply for lechery.

124–36   As soon as he takes Lucio aside, Claudio reveals his true nature: selfish, afraid of death and frustrated at the injustices of Angelo's new zeal to enforce the law. The two registers are central to the character and to the play's peculiar comic structure which finds absurdity in tragic situations. This dialogue is said out of the Provost's earshot. Now no longer on display to the city, Claudio becomes defensive and selfish. His explanation is full of special pleading and absent of contrite reflection.

In ll. 126–36, Claudio explains his problem in a matter-of-fact way. Rather unromantically, he describes his relationship with Juliet in business language: 'contract', 'propagation', 'dower', 'coffer', 'stealth'. Even their sexual relationship is rather oddly reduced to a 'mutual entertainment' (l. 135). These are not the words of a lover. Claudio was holding out for a better dowry (ll. 130–2). He alludes rather vaguely, and with a little bitterness, to Juliet's pregnancy, which, as it has become visible, has betrayed their relationship, ruining his plans for a good dowry and exposing him to the new laws (ll. 135–6). In effect, Claudio has been caught out on what should have been a good business deal. This is a rather different side Claudio to the one who earlier repented of too much liberty.

Claudio does not clearly say in l. 136 that Juliet is pregnant and may even nod slyly to the girl to make his meaning plain. Lucio gets it. The pregnancy is not welcome, as Claudio says in a half-line which completes Lucio's (l. 137).

137–56   Claudio complains irritably about the new laws and declares that Angelo must be either incompetent (l. 139) or asserting his authority (ll. 140–3). Claudio thinks himself a clumsy victim of this new regime who has been unfairly singled out for special punishment (ll. 146–50). He is correct, and Claudio feels victimized. He is being treated unfairly and made an example of. Lucio is also outraged but he seems not to take Angelo's laws very seriously. Claudio probably does not either. This is not a scene about a condemned man so much as an inconvenienced one. Lucio sensibly suggests appealing directly to the Duke, but Claudio has already tried that (l. 156).

157–67   Claudio asks Lucio to speak to Isabella on his behalf. This has been his real purpose all along. Claudio evidently has a good deal of confidence in Isabella's ability to persuade the Duke. We learn that she is about to become a nun, which gives Lucio's mission more urgency (ll. 158–9). The speech is insistent and hopeful. The veneer of humble repentance is gone: all Claudio's hopes rest with Isabella.

168–end of scene   Lucio readily agrees. He thinks Claudio's situation absurd: it is nonsense that he should be facing execution for a mere game. Shakespeare creates an interesting effect by contrasting the blank verse of Claudio's lines with Lucio's rough prose (Lucio speaks in verse later in the play). By speaking in prose, Lucio mocks Angelo's laws. However, he also (perhaps inadvertently) makes

Claudio look a little absurd for using poetic devices to ennoble what turns out to be, under Lucio's questioning, a fairly seedy affair (ll. 168–71).

Lucio exits in haste (l. 173). The Provost makes no verbal intervention to pull Claudio away (though he may make a gesture indicating his impatience), but it is Claudio who tells the Provost what to do.

Act I, scene iii

1–7　This scene starts in the middle of a conversation and explicitly so, for the Duke rejects something that the Friar has said (l. 1). What this is about soon becomes clear. The Friar has jumped to the conclusion that the Duke has got himself into trouble with a woman, i.e. the very thing that Claudio has been hauled off to prison for. The Duke wants sanctuary (l. 4), but he bristles at the Friar's supposition and insists that he has a serious motive (l. 6) The Duke is flustered and possibly even offended.

The Friar is a bit-part, a go-between, but much can be made of his *faux pas*; l. 7 is suggestive of both the curiosity of a gossip and the penitence of one who has already put his foot in his mouth.

8–18　The Duke's speech is mainly expository. He begins in a reassuring tone, talking to the Friar as if he were an intimate friend (ll. 8–11). The following lines are firmly controlled and the Duke seems confident about his plans (ll. 11–15). However, the next two lines are much more abrupt, as if the Duke is unable to sustain this intimacy (ll. 16–17). The Duke then prompts the Friar to interrogate him about his motives (l. 18). This is rather odd behaviour. The Friar is perhaps surprised to be asked to demand anything of the Duke, but he rather meekly assents (l. 18).

19–32　The Duke does not wait for the Friar to elaborate. This passage, full of complaint, is a nicely written vision of the city losing its grip on morality. The Duke admits his own responsibility for failing to enforce his own laws (ll. 20–4), although he mitigates this by using the royal 'we'. His sense of responsibility and disgust seems to be genuine. There is no humour; these are angry, trenchant lines.

Admitting his own failure, the Duke speaks with dark, apocalyptic words such as 'biting', 'weeds', 'terror', 'feared', 'dead'. The final lines (ll. 30–2) are hyperbole and suggest that the Duke's sense of what life is really like in the city is distorted.

The speech sounds like a soliloquy. The Duke is preoccupied with his own responsibilities and barely acknowledges the Friar, yet the Friar is there and has already been press-ganged into being the Duke's audience.

33–5   Although astonished by what he is hearing, the Friar is frank with the Duke, whom he berates for not enforcing the law himself (ll. 33–5). This is a gentle admonishment, but until now, the Duke has not been spoken back to.

35–55   In another long speech, the Duke continues to explain his motives to the Friar (and to the audience). In ll. 35–40, the Duke idiosyncratically insists that it would seem too heavy-handed for him to enforce the laws. In other words, he wants Angelo to do his dirty work for him, a point he affirms in ll. 41–4. The Duke is not a confident ruler and is clearly worried about what the people think of him.

The speech breaks at l. 44, when the Duke asks the Friar for a habit. As written, the implication is that the Duke and the Friar leave the stage to find such a costume, but many productions show the Friar finding a habit and putting it on the Duke as he speaks. Ll. 51–4 abruptly turn back to Angelo, whom the Duke ominously characterizes as a haughty, repressed zealot. The lines seem to be an afterthought, perhaps said as he and the Friar are leaving the stage. His final couplet suggests that he wants to test Angelo's probity (ll. 54–5).

Act I, scene iv

Although this scene has a serious point, it is potentially very funny. Lucio is out of his depth in the nunnery; he does not know how to behave and gets himself into trouble with Isabella. Isabella, not yet a full member of the order and still learning the rules, is given the responsibility of speaking to a visitor on her own: she is out of her depth too, as the nunnery is no more her world than it is Lucio's. A large part of the scene shows Lucio trying to persuade Isabella, and most of his strategies fail because Isabella does not share his feelings about Angelo. If anything, she approves of Angelo's crackdown on sexual misdemeanours. This exchange foreshadows Isabella and Angelo's two interviews, when Isabella will try to make the same kind of arguments that Lucio here uses on her.

1–14 Like the last scene, this begins in the middle of what is, we learn, a misunderstanding. Isabella has evidently been questioning Francesca about the restrictions she will have to commit to as a nun, but when she asks, apparently innocently, if the nuns live without any privileges (l. 1), Francesca assumes that Isabella is not happy with what she has so far heard and haughtily rebukes her (l. 2).

Francesca may be right; although Isabella hastily reassures the nun that she in fact craves stricter restraint (l. 4), she could easily be backtracking here, embarrassed to have been caught out by her own questions. Isabella can be played as a zealot who, much like Angelo, is obsessed with strict rules, but this reading risks limiting the character to a chilly stereotype. Her backtracking is comic, her zeal for strictness a little too eager to fully convince.

Lucio's offstage voice sends them into a panic. Francesca's exclamation that she hears a man's voice is funny *because* it is a man and she very abruptly leaves Isabella to deal with him alone, exiting the stage as fast as she can. (In Gibbons's edition, Francesca stays onstage, but many editors presume that she exits at this point.) This strikes me as more in keeping with the scene's comic tone: the scene is funnier if Francesca flees in half-panic and leaves Isabella alone. Francesca does not have any more lines in the scene so an exit is implied. Lucio continues to bang on the door and bellow throughout her speech, making her more anxious. Her last dizzying lines suggest haste (ll. 12–14).

15–16 Lucio is evidently still making a racket at the door because Isabella, now in charge, diplomatically tells him to shut up. She may well be concerned and nervous, but she still confronts him (l. 15).

Lucio's response is completely out of place in the nunnery (which is why it is funny). He cheerily greets Isabella and straight away questions whether she is still a virgin. Lucio's breezy manner is more suited to the city underworld. He bungles an attempt to flirt with Isabella, who may be offended (or just bemused) at having her chastity called into question. He quickly realizes his mistake and backtracks, praising her complexion (l. 16).

16–29 Not realizing that he is talking to Claudio's sister, Lucio puts his foot in it again, despite trying to be courteous, by talking of her brother (l. 21). Perhaps sensing he is in trouble (he had no such difficulties in his previous scene), Lucio tries to be both serious and light-hearted, but ll. 24–5 show him to be an inept bearer of bad news. His speeches become long-winded again, so Isabella naturally accuses him of teasing her (l. 29).

30–48 Lucio dances around the point with an even more elaborate and obscure unravelling of what could have been said in a few words. Ll. 39–44 are ludicrously inappropriate in a nunnery. His obsequious apology, in which he absurdly compares Isabella to a saint, only makes things worse. Isabella has to guess Lucio's meaning; the scene becomes another battle of wits, much like the game Lucio played with the two soldiers, except that this time Lucio is the loser. Isabella rightly guesses that Claudio has got Juliet pregnant.

Isabella calls Juliet her cousin and Lucio sounds surprised. His question at l. 46 is incredulous (or perhaps saucy), as he ponders the situation that Claudio and Juliet are in, being both cousins and lovers. Isabella's explanation (that 'cousin' is a term of affection) is a hasty correction and shows her embarrassment as she realizes what Lucio is thinking.

In terms of the story, Isabella's close relationship with Juliet is not important and never developed (and apparently forgotten by Act V). Theatrically, however, this little misunderstanding, on top of all the others, displays a crisis in communication: *Measure for Measure* is a world full of people who misunderstand each other. At l. 48, Isabella offer a simple solution, although the actress is entitled to measure it with as much desperation, impatience or frustration as she thinks appropriate.

49–71 Lucio is indignant and apparently slighted by the Duke's actions. He sounds rather conspiratorial in l. 50 as he explains to

Isabella why Claudio cannot marry Juliet, yet he immediately focuses on his own chances for preferment, which seem to be facing a setback under the new regime (ll. 51–2). The next lines reinforce the Duke's comment to the Friar that Angelo is a cold man who does not understand desire (ll. 56–63). In the final lines, Lucio presses his point hard. It is not just Claudio but the whole city that needs Isabella to intervene.

72–end of scene Isabella does not immediately respond but instead asks for a clarification; she can't believe that Claudio is to be executed. This is the first time that Claudio's sentence is clearly described. Lucio talks about the warrant he has seen (although he hasn't; possibly this is an action that can be worked into Act I, scene ii).

Lucio is a salesman, a persuader. He goads Isabella, using all his charm and rhetorical resources. This is Lucio at his most serious. He is right to sense that Isabella's power lies in her voice, although he may have in mind a more sexual meaning when he asks her to use her power to influence Angelo (l. 76). He dismisses Isabella's doubts. Isabella is fired up (ll. 83–5), but her final lines are politely measured.

ACT II

Act II, scene i

This scene develops two of the play's key themes: the exercise of justice and the relationship between authority and sexual deviance. Both are treated seriously in the opening exchange. Angelo, annoyed at having to defend himself to Escalus, explains why he cannot show Claudio any leniency. These same ideas are then explored comically.

1–4 The scene begins in the middle of a conversation, just like the previous two scenes. The officers are setting up the court; Angelo and Escalus are talking privately. In ll. 1–4, Angelo emphatically refuses to show any flexibility in the execution of the law. Presumably Escalus has asked him to show Claudio clemency. We are in the middle of an argument and Angelo seems to be getting

tired of it. These lines are didactic and emphatic. Although Escalus
probably started this conversation offstage, by giving the first line to
Angelo, Shakespeare makes sure that the audience's attention is
focused on him.

5–16 Escalus makes a genuine effort to persuade Angelo to be
more flexible, using a gardening analogy to convey the importance
of not being over-strict (l. 5). His next line sounds like a veiled warning; Escalus avoids being direct, his language and his manner maintain a level of deference as he diplomatically, and with great skill and
experience, attempts to tell Angelo that he is making a disastrous
mistake. Escalus wants to save Claudio because he knows Claudio's
father (l. 7), and presumably knows Claudio as well.

Nevertheless, Escalus cannot get Angelo to show Claudio any
special favour so he must try to win the argument on principle. Here,
Escalus oversteps himself. He wants to make the point that Claudio is
being punished for a crime that all men are guilty of, even Angelo.
However, Escalus cannot risk saying this directly so he creeps up to
the point in an elaborate 9-line sentence (ll. 8–16).

17–32 Angelo snaps back (ll. 17–8). Firm and impatient, he bristles
at the idea that *he* might be just as guilty of fornication as Claudio
and, further, demolishes Escalus' arguments by saying that the
probity of those who pass judgement is not an issue. His first point,
that thieves may be judged by juries that contain thieves (a point that
recalls Lucio's sanctimonious pirate), acknowledges authority's
weakness, but Angelo concedes only for effect. The law can only
judge those crimes that it knows about (this is what Angelo means
when he speaks of a jewel that is spotted in the ground, though this
is a curious analogy for crime), not those that are secret and yet to be
discovered (like the jewel that is trodden into the ground). This all
sounds weak, and it is. Angelo is not winning the argument and he is
angry with Escalus for pointing out inevitable flaws in any exercise of
authority.

However, Angelo's final point is important: he promises to
subject himself to the same punishment if he is found guilty of the
same crime (ll. 29–31). Angelo starts by talking about how 'we' must

treat the law, but as he gets more intemperate, his pronouns become personal: 'I that censure' and 'mine own judgement' (ll. 29–30). His final line in the speech is a brief statement which brooks no argument (l. 31). Escalus finally, reluctantly, defers to Angelo as if washing his hands of the matter (l. 32).

33–6 Angelo now clinches his point by curtly summoning the Provost and giving him an order to execute Claudio. He abruptly ends his conversation with Escalus to do so and his call for the Provost (l. 32) sounds tetchy, as if he is annoyed that the Provost is not there already (or it might be that he does not know who the Provost is). The execution order is businesslike; Angelo also instructs the Provost to arrange for Claudio to see his confessor. Sternly, Angelo adds that this is the only mercy he will show Claudio (l. 36). This severe comment is surely meant for Escalus as well as the Provost.

37–40 Escalus and (we shall later learn) the Provost are appalled by Angelo's detachment. Editors sometimes mark Escalus' world-weary meditation as an aside. However, he is not talking to himself so he is either addressing the audience, or someone else onstage, or Angelo, or he is just making a comment that can be heard by everyone. Angelo hears this, is meant to hear it: after all, Escalus is saying little more than he has already said to his face.

41–3 Elbow leads officers who have arrested Pompey on to the stage, changing the scene's tone from fraught argument to comedy. We can easily guess how the stage picture is formed here, for Elbow's commands, however backwards, are shouted at the officers who are presumably behind him – and the need to issue such commands suggests either that Pompey is reluctant to do as he is told, or that Elbow and the officers are being particularly aggressive, or a bit of both.

44–55 Annoyed at being interrupted, Angelo demands to know who Elbow is (l. 44). The question undermines Elbow's authority, but he quickly sets Angelo right. Elbow is an officious constable. He is overly deferential, as if unsure how many times to call Angelo his 'honour'. What he says is usually very different to what he means. He boasts that he leans on justice and scornfully calls his prisoners his benefactors (ll. 45–7).

Angelo is astounded and contemptuously corrects Elbow (ll. 48–9), who dodges the point by exaggerating the villainy of the two petty criminals he has arrested (ll. 50–3).

Escalus sees the joke and breaks Angelo's mood with a sarcastic remark (l. 54). The first two sentences in Angelo's next line are probably a response to this quip. Angelo then starts to press Elbow, who is for some reason (not explained in the text) suddenly speechless.

55–81   Pompey interrupts with a pun on Elbow's name. His interjection surprises Angelo, who now turns to questioning the tapster. It is only when Angelo starts interrogating him that Elbow finds his voice again. It should be apparent from ll. 58–61 that his antipathy towards Pompey is quite personal. Elbow has not simply arrested a malefactor, he has arrested someone he regards as a bitter enemy. His reasons soon become plain. Escalus picks up his reference to Mistress Overdone's brothel and in reply Elbow starts to talk about his wife (absurdly saying that he detests her when he means the opposite). It seems that it is the house itself which has excited Elbow so much. He keeps returning to the house, which he mentions with different adjectives six times and, whenever Escalus asks him for an explanation, he starts to talk about his wife.

Having started to question Elbow, Angelo is now silent and says little for the rest of the scene. Escalus takes on the role of interrogator. However, l. 81 is said to Angelo. Both are amused by Elbow and his prisoners.

81–5   Pompey takes charge and, evidenced by the length of his lines, he imposes his wit and personality on all around him. Next to him, Elbow is hapless. Pompey exploits Elbow's implausible verbal tick and, like Claudio before him, behaves more like the master than the offender. But unlike Claudio, Pompey's command is not secure; he elaborates to such an absurd extent that his meaning is as obscure as Elbow's. Having started out talking about Elbow's wife, Pompey digresses with a detailed discussion of different types of dishes.

86–102 Impatient now, Escalus tries to get Pompey to stop twittering (l. 86). In the following lines, Pompey manages to talk a good deal while saying nothing. He asks Froth to agree with him, but Froth must be a witless fool because Pompey is speaking nonsense. This is presumably a strategy; he is trying to talk his way out of his arrest and taking advantage of Elbow's inarticulacy to baffle Escalus.

103–6 Escalus briskly tells Pompey off and insists that he come to the point (ll. 103–5). Pompey's reply is a play on the sexual meaning of 'come'; Escalus acknowledges the pun, but he is not in good humour (ll. 106–7).

107–21 Pompey carries on as he did before, saying nothing with many words. The exchange is full of nonsense. Pompey subverts Elbow and plays interrogator, questioning Froth about absurd details, such as which day Froth's father died and which chair Froth likes to use.

Angelo finally loses his patience (ll. 118–21). He has been silent for some time, watching Escalus take charge of the investigation. Yet, with Pompey waffling and Escalus no closer to finding out what Elbow has charged Pompey with, Angelo ill-temperedly leaves the stage. He could have dismissed Elbow; that he does not do so shows that Angelo may be better at the theory of the law than its practice. His exit is cowardly: he is an inadequate leader, unable to take advice at the start of the scene, unable now to impose his will on the prating Pompey and baffling Elbow.

122–3 Pompey's bawdy interpretation of 'once' can be played two ways. Either he reacts as if her 'once' were her genitals; or as if she was promiscuous – or both. Elbow does not react to the insult.

124–40 Escalus is increasingly exasperated and bewildered by this strange pair of clowns. This time, Elbow is driving the comedy. Elbow pleads to Escalus and Pompey mocks him, then Pompey turns defence counsel, acting much like a barrister defending his client. He asks Escalus to look at Froth's face and the implication should be that Froth has an innocent face and would never do any wrong. Pompey subverts this expectation: if Froth's face is the ugliest thing about him, then he can't be responsible for anything uglier. Strangely, Escalus is taken in by Pompey's huckster logic (l. 140).

141–80 Now Elbow introduces real confusion by mixing up 'disreputable' and 'respected'. Pompey has fun, jibing that Elbow's wife is the most respected of them all, which Elbow takes as a slight against his honour and in angry protest gets himself into even more trouble. When Escalus interrogates Pompey, the tapster gets in another bawdy quip, that his Mistress was 'Overdone' by her last husband (l. 173). Escalus dismisses Froth: now he is alone with Pompey and Elbow.

181–219 Now Escalus shows off his wit as he compares Pompey (and his 'bum') to his Roman namesake, Pompey the Great. Sensing that he has gone too far, Pompey's reply is uncharacteristically brief and to the point (l. 191). Pompey rallies himself to argue that every young man will need to be castrated if the law is followed to the letter, but even so his reply remains brief and submissive.

Escalus' reply is authoritarian, even schoolmasterly. Yet Escalus lets Pompey go and with no clear reason, since his crimes seem to be at least equal to (if not more than) Claudio's. Escalus accepts that Pompey will never change and that arguing with him is exhausting and pointless. He may also agree that Angelo's severe enforcement of the law is unworkable. Pompey maintains his politeness, but in an aside mocks Escalus. Pompey retains his independence, his wit and his scornful attitude towards authority. Escalus has been duped.

220–end of scene Escalus either summons Elbow from the back or takes him aside. It is worth asking what Elbow has been doing over the last few lines: he was so upset before, it is hard to imagine how he would react to Froth and Pompey being sent away apparently without any penalty. Instead, his final lines are strangely muted and make no reference to what has just happened. With the Justice, Escalus brings the focus of the scene back to Claudio. Pompey's elaborate argument, though funny, has raised an important point. It leaves

Escalus (thinking more about Claudio than Pompey) troubled. Despondent, Escalus leaves, shaking his head at the world.

Act II, scene ii

1–2 The scene starts in the middle of a dialogue. The Provost has just asked to see Angelo. The case that Angelo is tied up with is presumably that of Elbow, Pompey and Froth.

3–6 The Provost's speech can be played as an address to the audience, but as we do not yet know whom he is talking about (but we may guess) the speech may be better played as a comment to himself. There is a risk the audience will be confused by the slide in pronouns: 'he' begins as Angelo, ends as Claudio. The passage is obscure and perhaps deliberately so, for its shifting focus reflects the Provost's anxious demeanour. In l. 5, the Provost unwittingly echoes Pompey's arguments in the previous scene.

7–17 Angelo enters, already irritated by Pompey, and briskly demands to know what the Provost wants. His impatience increases when the Provost makes a courteous but direct challenge to his authority (l. 9). This exchange repeats the opening of the previous scene (when Angelo argued with Escalus), only this time the temperature is raised, partly because Angelo is no longer addressing an equal but a subordinate.

L. 7 can be played as very tetchy, as in 'What do you want *now*?' But it can equally be played more sympathetically, though any sympathy must be quickly lost as Angelo effectively threatens the Provost with the sack: l. 13 is a reproach and a threat, as in 'do your job or resign'.

The Provost then reminds Angelo about Juliet (l. 16). Ll. 16–17 sound harsh and indifferent. Angelo seems to have no way of empathizing with Juliet, whom he speaks of as if she were cattle. His instruction to the Provost is not clear, it fails to engage with the problem at hand, and in his commands Angelo is neither decisive nor just.

18–27 The Servant brings news of Claudio's sister in language which sounds like a *double entendre*, for the woman 'desires access to'

Angelo (l. 19). Does Angelo begin to think about using Claudio to
seduce his sister this early? Angelo's question, though brief, is potentially very important. His curiosity is sparked and it is not the servant
he now speaks to, but the Provost. So – Claudio has a sister? The
implication hits home at once, there is a young woman over whom
Angelo already has a certain kind of power. How long does Angelo
take to ask this question? Until now Angelo has been impatient. Now
he is asking the Provost questions; he even asks him to stay. After
sending the servant away to fetch Isabella, Angelo seems to soften;
his new orders to look after Juliet are clearer and fairer.

The Provost presumably turns as if to leave, for Angelo tells him
to stay awhile (l. 27).

27–43 The scene's tone changes as soon as Isabella enters. We have
not seen Angelo courteous since the opening; now he greets Isabella
cordially (l. 27), and for much of these lines he just asks questions; it
is Isabella who dominates the dialogue. Isabella flatters Angelo and
dutifully humbles herself with deferential gestures. Angelo, we must
guess, watches – he is already falling for her and, as we have already
seen, he is very conscious of the sexual power his position gives him.

Isabella reluctantly pleads her suit as if she is merely discharging
her duty as a sister (ll. 30–5). Angelo is disingenuous: he knows full
well what Isabella's suit is but asks her anyway, and demands that she
follow protocol.

The Provost's brief prayer (l. 38) shows how poorly Isabella seems
to be doing, how badly she lacks the 'moving graces' needed to
convince Angelo. The Provost already knows that Angelo will not
respond to arguments; his hope, and Lucio's, is that Isabella will be
able to appeal to Angelo's sense of mercy. Lucio and the Provost are
anxious spectators; they do not stand together, but they frame the
stage, both hoping that Isabella will succeed, both despairing when
she falters.

Angelo puts the same arguments to Isabella as he earlier did to the
Provost and Escalus, but he is now polite, even paternal. Isabella is
upset but accepts the situation (too readily for the Provost and Lucio)
and even appears to praise a law which is 'just' even if 'severe' (l. 42).
Angelo and Isabella have a natural rapport, maybe even a sexual

chemistry. In l. 43 she gives up on Claudio in five words that recall Angelo's dismissive order to 'dispose of' Juliet some lines earlier.

44–57   Lucio now decides to intervene: the interview has not gone well, and Claudio appears to be lost. He either stops Isabella as she is leaving or rushes over to her, and he bluntly, urgently, persuades her to try again (ll. 44–8). These lines tell us much about what Isabella has not yet done: she has not knelt on the floor to entreat Angelo, she has not hung on his gown, she has spoken too moderately, she has been too humble and deferential. Lucio is desperate for Isabella to make things difficult for Angelo, to beat him down with feminine excess.

What does Angelo do during this aside? Chat with the Provost, go through the papers, stare after Isabella? At some point, Angelo starts to become infatuated with her; perhaps he has been so since her entrance.

Isabella starts to argue her case again, this time with more force: must he die? You *could* pardon him if you wanted to. In return, Angelo is more abrupt than he was before: he offers no more paternal explanations, he just repeats the same point: he will not release Claudio (l. 52).

Isabella and Angelo speak in half-lines, Angelo's refusals metrically completing Isabella's pleas. The pair are locked together in the blank verse's rhythms. Curt, officious, impatient, Angelo feels pestered and maybe a little pressured. Isabella's pleas have no reasoning to back them up; she even seems to agree with his arguments, but she continues to put pressure on Angelo like a petulant child.

58–67   Isabella catches Angelo's words and throws them back to him. She has reached her tipping point and now speaks at length, with anger. She hammers Angelo with four negatives (no, not, nor), and with each one pushes her argument forward with confidence. Isabella reacts to his officiousness by making an argument that is equal to his own: mercy is also a virtue of the powerful (a theme that the play will demonstrate in the final act and which is arguably its climactic moment, making this speech very important thematically). Then, in a brilliant conceit, she demands that Angelo think of himself in Claudio's place: even if Angelo would not commit Claudio's crime (a point later proved wrong), Claudio *would* show him mercy.

67–73 This is evidently too much for Angelo, who finally loses patience and comes close to losing his temper; l. 67 is abrupt, his earlier courtesy abandoned.

But Isabella will not leave: she has hit her stride and has another argument even more outrageous than the last. What if *she* were Angelo, and Angelo was Isabella?

How does Angelo react? Perhaps Lucio's aside at l. 72 is a clue – Isabella has hit a nerve, Angelo has no answer to her points, is clearly rattled. But Angelo is also developing an infatuation and it is Isabella's ability to speak thus that is part of that attraction. Is Angelo so rattled that he feels he can only contain her through despoiling her? Or is he genuinely falling for someone who resembles him so much?

Angelo has no immediate answer; instead he tries to dismiss Isabella by telling her that she is wasting her time.

74–84 Isabella raises the stakes by appealing to God and accusing Angelo of setting himself up as judge in God's place (ll. 74–81). She has overreached herself. Her point is not a convincing one and, spotting her weakness, Angelo continues with more confidence on the theme which he began in his previous line: it is the law, not the man, who condemns Claudio, i.e. Angelo is not taking responsibility but appealing to the 'law' instead (ll. 81–4). This is a good defence against Isabella's 'if you were him / if I were you' line of argument, but it is also officious and disingenuous. Angelo upsets Isabella (perhaps deliberately) by insisting that Claudio will be executed the next day (l. 84), which is sooner than she or Lucio expected.

85–90 Isabella reacts to this news. Her situation is now desperate and she pleads rather than argues with Angelo. She improvises frantic points, saying anything to change Angelo's mind: he's not ready for death (Barnadine will use this excuse later), it would disrespect heaven, no one has died, and so on. So anxious is she to influence Angelo that she even falls back on the argument that the crime is a common one.

91–2 Lucio's aside (l. 92) follows from this out-of-character point; Lucio is presumably thinking about himself.

93–108 L. 93 can be played as Angelo's annoyed reaction to Isabella's point, but his next words sound like a grudging admission. Angelo now broadens the question of empathy by asking her to think of all those who will sin if Claudio is not punished. The pendulum has swung back to Angelo and it is now he who has the running. All Isabella can now do is fall back on a plea for mercy (l. 103).

Angelo can again take the high ground. He returns to playing the part of a patient, paternal authoritarian. Angelo has recovered from the onslaught of Isabella's arguments and restored his sense of moral purpose. Nevertheless, in ll. 107–8 Angelo seems keen to end the debate.

109–13 But Isabella is not done yet. She makes a strategic retreat by appearing to acknowledge Angelo's argument (ll. 109–10), but then insists that it is Angelo and not 'the law' which gives the sentence and it is Claudio, not imagined people in the future, who will suffer. She then makes a good point that it is one thing to have power but another to use it like a tyrant.

That Lucio interjects approvingly here may well reflect an intended audience position, i.e. Shakespeare appeals to our sympathies here as well as making a subtle point about the difference between the theory and practice of power (l. 113).

114–29 Isabella's classical reference to Jove is an odd one for a nun to make, but she gets in a cutting remark about petty officers (l. 116), which undercuts Angelo's earlier pomposity and slyly characterizes him as officious.

Isabella develops her theme with steel and passion. She belittles Angelo's authority by reminding him that, despite his pride, his power will be short-lived (l. 121–2). This is Isabella's most significant victory yet and her success draws comment from both the Provost and Lucio. Lucio notices that Angelo is weakening (l. 129). The word 'coming' is also a sexual pun, and it may be that Lucio notices that Angelo is falling for her rather than her arguments. Angelo is falling in love with this strange woman who can win an argument lost by both Escalus and the Provost.

Isabella and Angelo will need to pause briefly to allow Lucio and the Provost their asides. The pause need not be a long one but it has to be explained, i.e. why does Angelo not respond, what are Angelo and Isabella doing? Is Angelo surprised, defeated, entranced? Or does he try to ignore her, busying himself with other tasks? Does Isabella expect a reply or is she drawing breath?

130–47   Angelo does not reply – perhaps he is unable to – so Isabella, now emboldened, starts on a different argument. She hits Angelo with a series of proverbs, the point of which is not immediately clear. This time, Isabella seems to speak over Lucio's enthusiastic interjections, which adds to the confusion.

This forces Angelo to break his silence. He protests that he does not understand the significance of these proverbs (l. 137). Isabella has been contrasting the different contexts of great men and ordinary men. Angelo's failure to understand this falls into her trap: Isabella demands that he look at his own desires (l. 143).

The point is a clincher; Angelo has no answer. In a brief aside, he confesses as much and even starts to realize that he is aroused by Isabella's victory (ll. 146–7). Aloud, he rudely dismisses Isabella and starts back towards his chamber. Though shaken, he still has power over Claudio and he reminds Isabella how dependent she is on him by walking away from her. Such dependencies can be exploited.

148–9   Isabella calls after him desperately. She is now worried that she has succeeded in humiliating the only man who can save her brother. Angelo stops and makes a surprising concession: he invites her to return the next day (l. 149). This is a short but significant line. It may be said quickly, even indifferently, but it is loaded. For Isabella, this means that she still has a chance and Claudio's execution has at least been delayed. Angelo has other ideas in mind. He is beginning to form a plan. Until now an audience might have thought only that Angelo has been rattled by Isabella's successful arguments; here we see in his words the first sign that his interest in Isabella runs in a different direction ('come again' replays Lucio's sexual pun, 'he's coming').

150–60　Still coy, Angelo carries on as if he is leaving, forcing Isabella to once again urge him to 'turn back'. Excited at this new concession, she offers a bribe. This pricks Angelo's interest (ll. 150–1) but Isabella is not about to offer herself, only her prayers. Ll. 154–60 are said with passion and fervour. Isabella can think of nothing better to offer him as a bribe than her prayers. These lines are an enthusiastic promise.

160–4　Angelo's reply (which completes Isabella's half-line) is deliberately ambiguous. The semicolon in l. 160 suggests a pause. Angelo is either amused by Isabella's excitement, or disappointed that she has nothing better to bribe him with. Either way, he clearly has hopes that their next meeting might yield better fruit.

　　Lucio recognizes that Isabella has done all she can and quickly tries to pull her away before she says something that will lose them this progress (l. 161). Isabella cannot help calling back to Angelo, who replies insincerely and then mutters a dark thought to himself (ll. 162–4). Yet Isabella is still not off the stage. Angelo is desperate to be by himself, but she comes back again, this time asking him what time she should come. He is relieved when she leaves, though she does not realize the irony of her farewell line (l. 166).

　　It is really not clear why the Provost leaves with them at this point, given that it was Angelo who asked him to stay: possibly Angelo nods to the Provost to escort the pair out. He is anxious to be on his own.

165–end of scene　Isabella leaves half a line hanging; when she is gone, Angelo softly completes it (l. 165). His reveals how much he wants her, even though he fears he will lose himself.

　　The next lines show Angelo's confusion. L. 169 signals a change in Angelo's thinking and is an opportunity for the actor to settle into the speech; the colon after 'not she' also begs a short pause before he launches on a self-reproach that is quite cutting. He compares himself to 'carrion' (l. 171) simply for finding her attractive – this is a man deeply troubled by his own desire, who gives himself no mercy. As the speech develops, Angelo starts addressing himself as someone else, someone he does not know. He interrogates himself much as he might have done Claudio, then as Isabella questioned him (ll. 180–1 directly echo Isabella's arguments).

There is urgency, desperation, *passion* in this speech of a kind that we have not yet seen in him. Angelo is clear that he has not been a hypocrite until now; he insists that he was never before attracted to a woman (l. 187). He is not a sexual opportunist. The feelings of sexual desire are new to him and they are frightening.

The speech continues, full of self-questions and doubts, Angelo's cool reasoning unloosened by his passion and self-loathing. When he reaches a climax Angelo spells out what he feels (ll. 189–90). A pause is natural here not just for the actor to draw breath but to take us to the final, curious line, which is almost but not quite a joke and gives us a little insight into Angelo's attitude to sexual desire, that he has not felt it before but often secretly wondered what it is like.

How does Angelo leave the stage? Maybe he starts to leave after 'quite' for the last sentence seems added on, an afterthought.

Act II, scene iii

This scene is both dark and funny. It is set in the prison, where the play's comic and tragic characters meet. The Duke is experiencing this dis-eased part of Vienna for the first time and arguably overreacts to Juliet, who he finds abandoned and pregnant in a prison, although she is not under arrest.

1–2   The Duke and the Provost enter the stage from different doors, the Duke calling across to the Provost. This is a test. The Duke is wearing his disguise for the first time, so he needs to be able to fool the Provost. The disguise works, but the Duke settles into it awkwardly and sometimes forgets himself. For example, in l. 1, the curious second clause might be played as a hurried afterthought. After confidently greeting the Provost (who he knows well), it must then occur to the Duke that the Provost will not recognize him – 'so I think you are', he adds, as a weak explanation of his apparent famil-iarity. The Provost is taken in and does not recognize him. The first test of the disguise is successful (l. 2).

3–9   This speech veers between the humility of a friar and the authority of a duke. The Duke cannot quite get the hang of not being a duke, but he also seems to relish the spiritual dignity that being a friar gives him. His first sentence sees him playing the part of the Friar, but he speaks awkwardly. His second sentence (ll. 5–8) is matter-of-fact and businesslike, more like the speech of a bureaucrat.

At l. 9, the Provost proves to be more than willing to let his prisoners have spiritual counsel. This is one of many lines which show the Provost to be a humane officer who worries about the welfare of his prisoners.

10–18   Juliet enters but stands in silence for several lines (she is waiting to hear from the Provost about what is going to happen to her). This is an opportunity for the Provost to help her, so he directs the Duke's attention to her. The Provost is compassionate and concerned. He is still angry about Claudio, so he is quick to complain about Angelo's unjust sentence to a stranger.

19–23   Prompted by the Provost, the Duke takes a keen interest in Juliet, who might wonder if she is about to be taken to a convent. His first question is straightforward, as is her answer (ll. 19–20). The Duke then proposes to test her penitence, and bluntly suggests that she might be putting it on (a rather hypocritical point for a disguised Duke to make) (ll. 21–3). Juliet's response is dutiful rather than enthusiastic (l. 24).

24–39   The Duke tells Juliet that her sin is greater than Claudio's. When Juliet agrees with this, the Duke starts to speak a convoluted, pompous sermon (ll. 30–4) which must try Juliet's patience, as she dares to interrupt him. Ll. 35–6 are perhaps a little indignantly spoken, as Juliet is clearly glad to be pregnant.

The Duke, unused to interruption and with no answer for Juliet, brings their meeting to an end. He tactlessly tells her about Claudio's imminent execution, which she seems to have been unaware of until now, and then leaves the stage, possibly anxious to get away from her.

40–end of scene　Upset to learn of Claudio's execution, Juliet speaks as an anxious, grieving lover. The Provost takes her offstage, perhaps comforting her. But the Provost is unable to offer any real solace, as it is he who will have to arrange Claudio's execution.

Act II, scene iv

This scene anchors the play – everything before has led up to it; everything that happens next follows from it. Angelo makes a critical departure from the role he has played so far. Yet there is potential for comedy, albeit uncomfortable comedy, as Angelo tries to find a way of broaching his bargain without saying plainly what he means. Isabella avoids Angelo's verbal traps. To what extent does Isabella understand or suspect what Angelo crudely hints at? Does she genuinely fail to recognize Angelo's not-so-subtle approaches, or is she already conscious that Angelo has sex in mind? Although these are lengthy speeches, there is potential for a lot of physical action as the cat-and-mouse seduction is played out. Angelo makes his intentions plain, Isabella tries to make him reflect on his hypocrisy, and then Angelo makes clear his bargain.

1–17　Angelo's second soliloquy picks up from the first and readies us for the second major scene between Angelo and Isabella. Although short, this speech gives us insight into Angelo's inability to cope with his feelings for Isabella.

The powerful inversions in Angelo's first line indicate his confusion. He is trying to explain himself to himself, incredulously assessing his predicament. He talks about himself as someone split in two, who says one thing but secretly longs to do the opposite of what he preaches. With l. 4, he seems to surprise himself when he says Isabella's name. His language is vivid, full of self-hate.

In ll. 4–7, he equates his hypocrisy with blasphemy and remarkably describes it in terms of consumption and pregnancy. Angelo is disgusted, but he is also relishing his disgust when he says words like 'chew' and 'swelling'.

Angelo's thoughts turn to what he was, to his career and his standing, but he confesses that he has grown tired of the law (ll. 7–9). This sudden insight prompts him to think of his own vanity. He admits that he enjoys seeming cold and aloof, though he would not say so to anyone else, but now wants to be a lover (ll. 9–12). The last four words of l. 12 lament the pressures of office. Angelo is burning to free his vanity and now seems contemptuous of his authority.

The second part of l. 15 is a strong statement and a key moment in the speech. Its meaning is ambiguous, but Angelo seems to be admitting that there is no difference between people of different ranks; 'blood' demands satisfaction. With his final lines, which hark back to Christopher Marlowe's *Dr Faustus* (when Faustus sells his soul to the Devil), Angelo shows how reckless he is and how far he is ready to go.

17–19 The Servant interrupts Angelo's thoughts. The last sentence of l. 17 is abrupt, Angelo is embarrassed and annoyed. However, he recovers himself when the Servant tells him that Isabella has arrived.

20–9 Excited but nervous, Angelo readies himself. He is overwhelmed by longing. He describes blood rushing to his heart (l. 20) and elaborates, trying to find a way to account for his feelings. But although Angelo tries to rationalize them, his feelings emerge in ripe, disruptive words such as 'blood' and 'offence'.

29–30 Isabella arrives, and Angelo stumbles a greeting. He recovers his former gravity and buries his frantic thoughts.

Isabella's greeting is unwittingly ironic. Angelo may take this as some encouragement.

31–40 Angelo begins with an ambiguous reference to Claudio's death, first insisting that he will die but then (confusingly) that he might live (l. 36). This is a significant concession, the first clue that there might be a way to save Claudio.

Angelo may mean this to be enough of a hint for Isabella to catch on that there is some negotiation to be done. But Isabella assumes that Angelo is offering to commute Claudio's sentence to life imprisonment (l. 37). She even tries to pin him down. This is the first of several exchanges in which Angelo tries to discreetly offer Isabella a chance to 'bribe' him and Isabella misunderstands him.

41–9   Angelo's next speech will sound obscure to modern ears and perhaps the best way to approach it is to make Angelo bluster. He loses his composure, but Isabella keeps hers.

50–4   Angelo recovers with a much more direct proposal: will Isabella allow to be done to her what Claudio did to Juliet? Even as he tries to seduce her, Angelo cannot hide his moral disgust, spitting words like 'stained' to describe sex (ll. 50–4).

54–5   Is he being serious? Is he testing her? Isabella is unsure, but she is assertive in her response, insisting that she values her soul over her body (ll. 54–5).

56–60   This annoys Angelo, who retorts dismissively that Isabella's soul is not important and then tries to make a bureaucratic point that Isabella will not be responsible for a sin that she is forced to commit (l. 56). Isabella is surprised and perhaps offended at this extraordinary turn in Angelo's argument (l. 57) and Angelo immediately backtracks, perhaps embarrassed, perhaps himself shocked by his own remarks. Instead, he awkwardly claims that he is merely testing Isabella (ll. 58–60).

60–4   Angelo is drawing close to propositioning Isabella, but he is not yet ready for it. Isabella's directness has caught him by surprise. Now he continues stealthily, pretending to make a false argument. Ll. 61–2 pompously remind Isabella that he is in charge, that Claudio's life hangs in the balance. The following two lines are said in a different key: having established his authority, Angelo now seems to undermine it by coaxing Isabella to seduce him.

64–8   Isabella either ignores this hint or she simply misses it. She thinks the sin Angelo means is that of pardoning Claudio, so she happily agrees (ll. 64–6). In a rather sinister couplet, Angelo uses her words against her. He is trying to trap her into giving herself to him and at this point seems to assume that Isabella has caught his meaning (ll. 66–8).

69–73   However, Isabella now makes it clear that the only sin which is pardonable is that of begging for Claudio's freedom.

73–5   This is very frustrating for Angelo, who demands to know if she is being crafty or just stupid. These lines are vicious and ill-tempered. Angelo is running out of patience.

76–7   At the same time, Isabella's staunch virtue excites Angelo even more. Isabella humbly pleads ignorance. These lines can be played as written; they are straightforward enough. However, it is possible to start introducing some complexity into Isabella's role. Maybe she has caught a sense of what Angelo is up to, or she is at least beginning to suspect that his tests are not altogether sincere. Isabella's situation is a dangerous one.

78–83   Although rarely marked as such, these lines could be said as an aside. It is the first time Angelo has talked so directly about Isabella's beauty. Yet these lines are more of accusation than a compliment. In l. 81, Angelo firmly tells Isabella to pay attention. If she is finding it difficult to follow him, he will be clearer about his purpose.

83–98   Angelo takes Isabella through the situation with the precision of a legal counsel. Proposition 1: Claudio is going to die (Isabella agrees). Proposition 2: his punishment is lawful and appropriate (not sure where this is leading, Isabella agrees). With these fundamentals clearly established, Angelo describes a moral problem. If there were someone who could influence the law to save Claudio, would Isabella offer herself to that person?

This is an appallingly inept seduction. Angelo's language is legalistic and formal; he uses phrases such as 'this supposed', 'subscribe not that', 'credit', and so on. He even uses the word 'accountant'.

Still too nervous of directly implicating himself in this hypocrisy, Angelo also distances himself in his hypothesis: it would not be himself, but someone who has 'credit' with him, that he imagines Isabella seducing.

99–104   This speech is rich in dramatic irony. Isabella may intend to answer Angelo in strong terms, but the words she uses heighten the erotic tension of the scene. Angelo may listen to her with increasing excitement as she talks of being whipped and lying naked on a bed, longing for pain. Is Isabella herself entirely innocent or is she (however subconsciously) responding to Angelo's sadism?

105–12   Angelo is putting pressure on Isabella now by using Claudio's life as leverage. Ll. 105–6 lend themselves well to a range of different readings. Angelo could be dismissive, forcing Isabella to come to him. Alternatively, Angelo could look Isabella straight in the eye, testing her. Isabella may respond with confidence, even passion; but l. 106 could also be said in a faltering way, Isabella looking at Angelo for the first time with some understanding of his real purpose.

Isabella answers Angelo by talking about herself and Claudio in abstract terms (a brother, a sister). She clings on to the fiction that Angelo is disputing a moral position. Angelo is dogged, he presses her further, he thinks he has her in a trap and his confidence is growing (ll. 110–12).

112–21   Isabella is more than a match for Angelo: she parries his accusation that she is as hard as he by refusing to compare a free pardon with one obtained through corruption (ll. 112–13). The purity and intelligence of her answers probably only make Angelo want her more and by matching his arguments so well; Isabella boxes him into a corner: Angelo has to become blunt if he is to achieve his purpose.

Angelo tries to make the point that it is Isabella's fault that he desires her so much. He starts to get more aggressive; unable to say what he wants to say directly, Angelo becomes ever more impatient at Isabella's (to him) willful refusal to get his point (ll. 115–17).

Isabella's response is conciliatory and apologetic. She styles herself a hypocrite for asking leniency for a crime she hates, but balances love and hate to excuse herself. Once again, her lines can be misread (or they betray her). What is it that she hates, who does she love? She means (superficially at least) Claudio, but Angelo's mind runs in a different direction.

122–4 In l. 122, Angelo encapsulates the argument that has been put to him again and again. Wasn't it Isabella who told him to look within himself for a fault like Claudio's? Either Isabella is completely innocent, still thinking a trial is being made of her virtue, or she is desperately trying to turn the conversation around.

Isabella takes this line as an admission – Angelo has the same weakness as Claudio. She continues, talking about principles and moral dilemmas, but each time she evades Angelo's purpose, she forces him to be more blunt and aggressive.

125–39 L. 125 is a very direct hint. Isabella gives a conventional answer, admitting that her sex is inconstant and credulous. But here she finally falls into Angelo's trap. He has admitted he shares Claudio's desires; now he takes these lines as evidence that Isabella does as well. Angelo moves straight to the point and now becomes insistent, even threatening. He turns his seduction into an arrest (ll. 132–5); she has been trapped by her own arguments (l. 132). When he demands that Isabella put on 'the destined livery' (l. 139), i.e. become his (sexual) servant, his purpose is utterly clear. Isabella cannot ignore this.

140–4 Horrified, Isabella tries to placate him with mild flattery as if she were trying to calm a wild animal (ll. 140–1). But Angelo cannot be tamed: encouraged, he now says exactly what he feels and what he wants (l. 142).

Isabella is shocked, but she has a powerful comeback: doesn't Claudio love Juliet? Despite everything, she holds on to her mission to save Claudio; she stays within the terms of the debate which Angelo is now trying to rip apart. Indeed, his hypocrisy strengthens her point (ll. 143–4).

145–54 Now Angelo makes the situation absolutely clear: he may say that he loves her, but what he actually wants is a straight exchange: Claudio will live if Isabella will sleep with him (l. 145). These are quick lines. The tension has broken, the argument is no longer a hypothetical one and the performance will naturally turn more physical and desperate.

At first Isabella doesn't believe him, she thinks this is some kind of test, but when Angelo insists, Isabella seems to lose her temper (l. 151). She stands up to him and threatens to expose his true character to the world (l. 154).

155–61 Angelo, however, has the upper hand: who will believe a young woman over a deputy? Isabella is destroyed, he thinks, and now nothing holds him back. L. 155 is a cruel, mocking line. Angelo sneers Isabella's name and then tries to suffocate her with words. He imagines her stifled, stinking of corruption, her reputation ruined. With the second part of l. 160, Angelo seems to let go of his cold demeanour entirely and even describes himself as someone who has given free rein to his desires. These lines' power lies in Angelo's transformation and Isabella's reaction. Angelo has been edging away from his former self since the scene began, but now he holds nothing back. He should appear possessed and on the edge of violence.

162–71 This speech is angry, aggressive, biting, unrestrained. Isabella says nothing back. He could be about to rape Isabella, but he doesn't. Instead he reiterates what she must do to save her brother. If Isabella doesn't sleep with him, Claudio will not only die, but his death will be drawn out. His parting shot is a threat but it is also a challenge (l. 171). Angelo has had enough of Isabella's stubbornness, is impatient at being defeated in questions of law and moral argument.

Why does Angelo leave now? The trajectory of the scene so far is towards rape, and some productions make the scene violent, but Angelo does not want to use physical force to get what he wants; his tactic is to use his authority to dominate Isabella. Many actors turn the end part of the scene into a physical enactment of implied rape in which Angelo only just holds himself back. There is a reason why he stops short of rape, why he doesn't have her there and then. It is not enough to have her; she has to give herself. He is both angered and turned on by her virtue. And, in his own warped way, Angelo is actually quite sincere when he says 'I love you', but he knows no other way to express that desire than through domination. Isabella is forceful when she thinks she has got something on him, but it is her claimed victory that makes Angelo snap. She thinks she's won and he can't bear it. Isabella is a strong character, but she is momentarily subjugated, humiliated, violated.

172–end of scene   L. 172 is a plea that no one hears. Isabella is shaken and desperate. She is also angry; she sees through Angelo's hypocrisy with the horror of one who had always, until now, respected authority. Her one hope is that her brother will prove a more honourable man than Angelo (l. 180). Surely, even though Claudio is in imprison for fornication, he would gladly volunteer for death to save her honour? The question she begins with shapes her thinking. She needs to speak; moreover she needs to find a way of getting rid of the responsibility that Angelo has given her.

This speech is an important set-up for the next scene. Of course Isabella is naive to think her brother is capable of such selflessness, but at this point delusion is all she has. Claudio is the only person who can relieve her of the responsibility which Angelo has left her with and he can only do that by willingly offering to put her honour before his death. Isabella is clinging to a lie.

ACT III

Act III, scene i

This scene, which comes at nearly halfway through the play, is a fulcrum where different plots come together. Several questions are raised that the play never answers. The Duke may be disguised, but he could at any time resume his office and simply release Claudio. This is his first and in many ways most substantial and intimate scene with Isabella, yet he ends the play by taking her as his wife.

1–4   The scene starts with the Duke, who enters with Claudio and the Provost. The Provost may enter from a different door or he may be escorting Claudio. The Duke must enter with Claudio as his first two words indicate that he and Claudio are in the middle of a dialogue. As Shakespeare's stage had no way of discovering actors already onstage, they walk on together. However, in modern theatres it is possible to fade lights up on this scene, with Claudio confined in his prison cell.

The Duke, acting as Claudio's confessor, asks him a question without appreciating its dramatic irony: Claudio is hoping for a pardon, which means he knows that Isabella has gone to see Angelo and he is now anxiously waiting for news. He seems to be confident, which is why he boldly asserts that he is ready for death (l. 3). We will learn later how little Claudio is really ready to die. He is not completely sincere.

5–43   In this pompous, convoluted speech, the Duke says little that is of real comfort to Claudio. The Duke is playing his part and he seems to enjoy it, as the speech goes on for more than thirty lines. Yet it is composed of little more than a series of mottos about living and dying. He makes no attempt to offer Claudio spiritual comfort. Some productions shift the emphasis of the performance on to Claudio, who is too preoccupied with his own fate to listen to the Duke's self-regarding sermon.

There are some powerful lines in the speech: ll. 19–21, for example, raise questions about the self which echo Angelo's earlier insight into *his* divided mind. Even so, the speech is an oddly inappropriate one for a friar to deliver to a condemned man. The Duke does not talk about God, sin or salvation. Instead, he endeavours to persuade Claudio that he is missing nothing by dying young. Old age is full of indignity and Claudio is best off without it.

Claudio speaks bravely, but he has yet to hear news from his sister. His mind is elsewhere (ll. 40–3).

The Provost has no lines. Visually, he reminds the audience that the scene is set in a prison. He may watch Claudio, but as confessions are usually private he might better be employed elsewhere on the stage.

44–9   The news Claudio has been waiting for arrives almost as soon as he stops speaking: Isabella calls from offstage (her lines are meant to echo Lucio's in Act I, scene ii). She is polite, but she is trying to get attention. Shakespeare writes Isabella's entrance as a parallel action. On one side of the stage, the Duke continues to give Claudio his confession; on another, the Provost answers Isabella's calls and admits her to the prison. Claudio does not hear Isabella; he does not know she's arrived until l. 49 when the Provost brings her over to her brother.

50–3 As Isabella goes to her brother (and presumably embraces him), the Duke steals the Provost away for a private word. Suddenly, the scene becomes conspiratorial. The Duke is quick. He may have thought to spy on Isabella when she arrived (his first line in the scene hints that Claudio has just told him about Isabella). More in keeping with his character would be to show the idea as a sudden one, as though it just occurred to him. The Duke and the Provost hide, but they should still be visible to the audience.

54–60 Isabella has come to prepare Claudio for death but she needs him to first release her from the burden placed upon her by Angelo. Claudio is waiting to hear if Isabella has managed to plead successfully for his life. In l. 54, he is eager to know if Isabella has won him a pardon. Isabella's response dodges his question. She repeats 'most good' in l. 55 because she is nervous, not sure how to tell her news.

A pause seems warranted before the next line. Isabella is being disingenuous but lying does not become her. She briskly tells Claudio that his execution is set for the next day, but she is obviously hiding something.

61–9 Claudio immediately senses that Isabella is not telling him everything, so he pushes her for more details about her audience with Angelo (l. 61). What follows is a fraught exchange, as Isabella seeks to subtly reveal the truth. Like Angelo, she skirts around her true meaning as she tries to find a way of conditioning Claudio's response. Claudio's mind runs in a different direction and he resists making it easy for his sister even when he begins to suspect the truth.

Although brief, Claudio's responses are important. To begin with, he says little, interjecting one-line questions that are at first optimistic and then almost sarcastic.

L. 60 may be a resigned comment, but it may be desperate; with l. 62 Claudio leaps on Isabella's hint that there might be a way to escape death. Claudio grabs hold of this, but does not question *whose* heart might be at risk.

He misinterprets Isabella's next lines: she tells him that Angelo's pardon will come at too terrible a price, but Claudio thinks that she means life imprisonment (l. 66).

Isabella vacillates and avoids the issue (ll. 67–9), Claudio presses her to explain what she means (l. 69) – whether he shows it outwardly or not, he is anxious.

70–2 Isabella sets a trap not dissimilar to the one that caught her in the previous scene. Claudio's honour is at stake. However, he is impatient (and desperate), so he demands that Isabella explain herself (l. 72).

73–80 Isabella dodges Claudio's demand by questioning his courage. Isabella gives something away in l. 73: she doesn't fear *for* Claudio, she is frightened *of* him. She *needs* Claudio to insist that he would rather be executed than see his sister dishonoured, because if he doesn't then the responsibility to stand up to Angelo becomes hers. But she quakes because she suspects that Claudio might not prove to be a better man than Angelo. At the same time, she is exaggerating for rhetorical effect and it is a trick she has learned from Angelo. Angelo's strategy was to get Isabella to agree a principle so that it would be hard for her to refuse him when he made his proposition. Now Isabella tries the same trick with Claudio. Is he man enough to die (l. 76)? Is he a giant or a beetle (ll. 77–80)?

80–4 Claudio falls for it. Pathetically, he takes offence at being compared to a beetle and angrily protests that he is ready to embrace death – but this is pure bravado.

85–7 Isabella is excited. Not only does Claudio seem to live up to her expectations of what a man should be, but the moral responsibility will be taken away from her when she explains why it is that she can't save him. Yes, Claudio will die; he is far too good a man, much better than the hypocritical Angelo.

88–94 L. 88's 'outward-sainted deputy' sounds as if it should be said with a certain amount of revulsion. Having enthused about Claudio's nobility, Isabella gets sidetracked into a bitter rant about Angelo, who is 'fowl' (in the avian sense, but the other sense is meant too), a 'devil'; he is 'filth', he belongs in 'hell'. To anyone but Isabella, this sudden tirade, from a novice nun, is a surprise. She is caught up in her own anger and forgets that Claudio knows nothing of Angelo's real nature.

Naturally, Claudio is taken aback and suspects that Isabella is not telling him everything. In l. 94, he registers his surprise – does she really mean Angelo?

95–8 Oh yes, *Angelo*. Isabella continues her rant, mocking the idea that Angelo is 'prenzie' (this means 'princely', which is an acceptable substitution for modern audiences and is preferred by some editors). Now firmly confident that Claudio shares her anger and her values, Isabella tells him about Angelo's proposition.

98–105 Having spoken wildly when his masculinity was challenged earlier, Claudio is now mainly silent. L. 98 is surely ironic – Isabella takes him to mean, 'How outrageous, I'll never consent to that!' But Claudio is really saying, 'My God! I'm going to be free!'

Then the truth dawns on Claudio (l. 102). Isabella takes this as the affirmation she has been looking for, but the line is actually Claudio's realization that 'Oh, you're not going to do it, are you?' His next line (l. 105) is more like a 'thanks, but no thanks' or 'thanks for nothing', grudging rather than gracious.

106–10 L. 106 is insistent: there is no debate. Claudio cannot help but agree with his sister, but he is busy trying to collect his thoughts about this extraordinary turn of events. All of a sudden, there is a way to avoid being executed. All he needs to do is persuade Isabella to set aside her high principles for a moment.

L. 107 begins with a single-word sentence which begs a following pause. This is the point where Claudio must steer the conversation in a different direction.

He is clumsy, though. He pretends to share her outrage, noting that Angelo is committing the same crime that he is being punished for. But in ll. 109–10, Claudio puts forward a different view. Echoing a point that Angelo also made, he ventures that it would not be sinful for Isabella to sleep with a man if he forced her to.

111–15 Isabella is shocked and confused. What does Claudio mean? This is *not* going according to the script. Now it is Claudio's turn to unburden his fears on his sister. Surely, he says, a little sex for his life can't be so sinful, because Angelo is wise and would not risk eternal damnation for a fleeting affair? This is desperate, and Claudio seems to realize this in l. 114, when he runs out of argument (Claudio is not really much of a debater) and falls back on an exclamation. Isabella's reply is impatient.

116–17 These two lines, which grate against each other, articulate the play's moral dilemma with bleak clarity. Where do they go from here?

118–32 In this superb speech, Claudio's pretended steadfastness, his supposed readiness for death, ebbs away completely. In this terrifying passage, Claudio is not melancholic, he is distressed. It is vital that Claudio impress on Isabella how important it is she help him, but Claudio is not calculated, he is deeply emotional. His fear is primal, beyond reason, hence his violent and restless words: 'howling', 'ache', 'loathed', 'viewless', 'horrible', and so on. Any kind of life is better than death.

132–6 L. 132 is more a prompt to the actress than a line. Isabella is appalled, devastated. Claudio is now begging her (l. 133) and he tries again to convince her that she would not be committing a sin. Frantic as he is, Claudio is not only thinking about his own life. He finds it utterly incredulous that for such a simple thing as sex Isabella will not save him. Claudio is a wastrel from a city comedy, Isabella a heroine from a tragedy. She is high-minded, he is realistic and down-to-earth: he is only in prison at all because he was trying to negotiate a better dowry before marrying Juliet. For Isabella, 'virtue' is absolute; for Claudio, it is relative to the situation.

136–44 Isabella is furious. Her first two lines are insults; she then calls Claudio's manhood into question again and accuses him of incest for wanting to live by her dishonour. She virtually calls him a bastard (having before praised him for being like their father) and disowns him.

Yet her anger is misplaced. What she says to Claudio now is what she should have said to Angelo before, and in the second sentence of l. 143 she even seems to confuse the two. Isabella's main hope has been that Claudio would be too noble a man to allow her to corrupt herself, but now Claudio is pressing her to go back to Angelo and bargain for his life, he is no better than the Deputy – that is why Isabella spits defiance at her brother rather than Angelo.

144–7 Isabella's final four lines in this speech are cruel (ll. 144–7). Isabella refuses to help Claudio and even says she will pray for his death. She can be as cold and hateful as Angelo.

148–51 Despite Claudio's desperate pleas to 'hear me', Isabella continues to criticize his crime and, in l. 151, again looks forward to his death. These are not just angry words; they are the last words she might ever say to him. In fact, they *are* the last words that Isabella speaks to Claudio in the play.

151–3 These are action lines. There are several ways of performing them. Isabella could be about to say more to Claudio, the Duke rushing to intervene before she says anything else that she will regret. Alternatively, she could start to leave after l. 151, angry and upset, Claudio calling after her, the Duke rushing to catch her. Something prompts the Duke to expose himself. Whatever action is chosen, this is a chaotic moment, a crisis point, which forces the Duke to intervene.

153–8 The Duke's sudden appearance is a surprise to Isabella, who has not met him before. His lines are said hastily. Isabella is still angry, Claudio still calling for her. The Duke has to stop Isabella and calm Claudio down. Though she is talking to a friar, Isabella is too upset to be anything but blunt and a little suspicious (l. 153). The Duke quickly tries to persuade her to wait a moment for him so that he can talk to her. Isabella tetchily replies that she has no spare time, that he will be stealing her time, but she assents even so. He is a friar after all. She waits elsewhere on the stage, perhaps resenting the Duke's intervention.

159–75   The Duke boldly admits that he has been listening to the siblings and convinces Claudio that Angelo is merely testing Isabella's virtue. There is no real hope. Again, these are hasty lines. The Duke is thinking quickly because he does not want to keep Isabella waiting. He persuades Claudio by lying that he is Angelo's confessor. With such lies, he calms Claudio, who now asks if he can apologize to his sister. The Duke stops him (he is deliberately keeping the pair apart) and then persuades the Provost to leave him alone with Isabella. The Duke is astonishingly direct with the Provost. L. 172 is abrupt and officious, more the words of a duke than a friar, yet the Provost accepts and takes Claudio offstage. The Duke has now cleared the stage for his scene with the young novice.

176–83   The Duke's first lines to Isabella are meant to be flattering and said in the key of a concerned friar. Although written in prose, ll. 176–9 have an iambic rhythm that is meant to be consoling. They are a preface to the Duke's main point: he wants to know what Isabella intends to do.

184–98   Though less upset, Isabella remains determined to expose Angelo to the Duke when he returns. The Duke immediately sees the flaw in her plan: Angelo will simply say that he was testing her. The Duke now promises Isabella that Claudio can be saved without Isabella losing her honour and reputation. In this passage and several more in this scene, the Duke is long-winded. Even so, he has Isabella's interest, as she asks to hear his plan. Despite what she said to Claudio before, she still wants to save him (ll. 197–8).

199–213   This passage and the next are largely expository, as the Duke explains to Isabella that there is another woman who has been treated badly by Angelo. Isabella will be curious if a little confused at l. 202, but the Duke soon explains that Angelo and Marianna were betrothed, that a shipwreck cost Marianna her brother's life and her dowry, and that Angelo coldly broke his promise to marry her as a consequence. The parallels between Marianna and herself strike Isabella immediately. Both have lost a brother; both have been treated contemptuously by Angelo. Isabella may not notice the parallel between Angelo and Claudio, both of whom put their prospective dowry before love. Isabella must find this extraordinary. What does the Duke think? Has he had his doubts about Angelo's character all along?

214–25   The Duke's language is awash with metaphors. He's already talked about the sea; now he talks of tears (twice), of washing and of lamentation. This seems to be a strategy to engage Isabella's sympathies and it seems to work. Isabella's questions prompt the Duke to continue his story and each time she makes a comment, she seems to identify closely with Marianna. Having coaxed her with vivid story-telling, the Duke then tells Isabella that she has an opportunity to help Marianna and Claudio at the same time. This is important. Since her soliloquy at the end of Act II, Isabella has felt powerless, her faith in authority and family damaged. Naturally, she wants to know how she can help and when she asks, she calls the Duke 'good father', the first time she has spoken to him with such respect (l. 225).

226–42   Now the Duke explains his plan. He wants to swap Isabella for Marianna in Angelo's bed. It is a dangerous plan, but Isabella is listening intently. Though a longish piece of prose whose main purpose is to set the scene for the next part of the narrative, this is a vivid speech. The Duke twice uses sentences with several clauses to put into sequence a series of events: Isabella will go to Angelo, Marianna will take her place, Claudio will be saved, and so on. The Duke is persuasive. It all sounds so simple.

243–end of scene   Undaunted, Isabella agrees to the plan. There is hope after all. So little does she worry about the evident dangers that she either places absolute trust in the Duke or she enjoys the risk. The Duke seals the agreement and sends her back to Angelo. He is himself about to leave when he is waylaid by Elbow.

Act III, scene ii

Act III, scene ii is a run-on scene. The Duke stays onstage to see Elbow and the others entering.

1–4   Elbow and Pompey are arguing when they enter. In the first line we hear, Elbow insults Pompey's profession by accusing him of buying and selling people. Although Elbow is in some respects a stereotypical comedy policeman (similar to Dogberry in *Much Ado About Nothing*), some of his language is not simply comic. These are nasty lines: he talks of beasts and bastards, and this time he does not use the opposite words to say what he means.

He and Pompey obviously make a racket as they enter the prison, and must be together an extraordinary sight. The Duke is astonished (l. 4). Despite his urgent mission to see Marianna, he stays to find out more about these clowns (unlike Angelo, who did not have the patience to suffer them).

5–9   Pompey has a thick skin. He doesn't rise to Elbow's insults; instead he picks up on the idea that he buys and sells people and laments that the world allows commerce but condemns his trade. He is irrepressible.

10–15   Elbow senses that Pompey is stalling and brings him on towards his cell. This is when he spots the Friar. This is another test of the Duke's disguise. In his greeting (l. 11), the Duke seems to affectionately mock Elbow's unusual way of talking. Fortunately, Elbow misses the jibe. The Duke now asks the same question that Angelo put to Elbow in Act II. The Duke gets a much more straightforward answer. Pompey has been arrested for possession of a picklock.

16–30   In l. 16, the Duke mocks Pompey but he is probably also mocking Elbow. The Duke's language is strong: he tells Pompey off in colourful language that can be relished for comic effect in words such as 'abominable', 'beastly' and 'stinkingly'. It is hard to judge from the text alone whether the Duke is genuinely outraged by Pompey or whether he is, on some level, enjoying the opportunity to make the poor tapster squirm. Pompey starts to reply as he usually does with an elliptical retort, but the Duke is having none of it; he cuts Pompey off (a rare feat) and waves at the officer to take Pompey into the prison, perhaps forgetting for a moment that he is not the Duke.

31–8 Elbow and the Duke talk about Pompey as if he is not there, Elbow tactlessly boasting about the length of the rope which will hang him (l. 36). Pompey is rattled, which is unlike him; when he sees Lucio enter (as Elbow and the Duke talk), he sees an opportunity to escape.

39–46 Pompey hopes for the kind of support and concern that he earlier saw Lucio give to Claudio. But Pompey is not Claudio, and Lucio refuses to take the situation seriously; in fact, he thinks it funny to see Pompey arrested and wastes no time in mocking the poor tapster for his predicament. Lucio even ridicules Pompey's name (l. 40). Lucio batters Pompey with cruel questions. Pompey is (for once) silent, refusing to be drawn by Lucio's barbs.

47 The Duke wryly comments on Lucio's performance. This might be an aside, said either to himself or to the audience. There is no reason for Lucio to stop badgering Lucio, so this line is perhaps best spoken quickly.

48–67 Lucio continues to tease Pompey. Enjoying Pompey's discomfort, Lucio goes further and demands that the pimp be sent to prison. This is a funny yet nasty exchange; Lucio needles Pompey and seems to enjoy it. Why is Lucio so vicious? There is nothing in the text that really explains Lucio's behaviour. He may be deliberately distancing himself from Pompey to avoid being charged himself, or he may simply dislike the tapster.

67–76 Lucio has so far ignored the Duke, but he now greets him just to annoy Pompey (ll. 67–8). However, Lucio cannot resist another quip at Pompey's expense. He greets the Duke politely, then flings scabrous insults at Pompey (l. 70). There is a brief amount of confusion, with Lucio turning his back on Pompey to talk to the Duke, Elbow pushing Pompey onwards, Pompey calling once more to Lucio, this time recognizing that Lucio will not help him (l. 72). As Pompey is led offstage, Lucio divides himself again between the Duke, whom he courteously asks for news, and the wretched Pompey, at whom he barks one more insult.

77–81   The Duke is conscripted into a conversation with Lucio, but Lucio immediately catches his interest (and his vanity) by asking for news of the Duke. Disingenuously, the Duke pretends to know nothing and then asks a leading question to see what Lucio understands, and will say, about his alter ego (ll. 77–8). Lucio's next line may be said either with concern or bewilderment. The Duke's absence mystifies him. He does not realize the irony of his next question, but the Duke does. He feigns a little indifference and gives an incurious answer, of the kind that he might have expected Lucio to provide (l. 81).

82–99   Lucio now rewards the Duke's selfish interest with a little tirade that probably astonishes the Duke, who had no idea that his absence would provoke such outlandish opinions. Lucio petulantly criticizes the Duke, but the real target of these lines is Angelo, whose new strict regime he resents (ll. 82–4). The Duke bristles at this affront to his judgement so, despite what he has just heard from Isabella, he feebly defends Angelo (ll. 85, 88).

Lucio, however, seems to take these comments as more grist to the mill, and he continues to blather about Angelo, even calling into question whether he is human. So eager is Lucio to unload his annoyance that he enlists the Duke as a confidant even though he is a stranger (ll. 89–93). The Duke finds it hard to take Lucio seriously and so prompts him: if Angelo is not human, than how was he born (l. 94)? Lucio's explanation is both witty and hyperbolic. He turns from Angelo's birth to his bowel movements. This is a speech which the Duke evidently enjoys (l. 99).

100–15   So long as Lucio is criticizing Angelo, the Duke enjoys his wit. However, Lucio now turns on the Duke and at this slander the Duke grows ill-tempered as he listens to his outrageous claims. Ironically, Lucio thinks he flatters the Duke and starts to talk about him as a contrast to Angelo. The Duke would never have sent men to their deaths for fornication, he boasts (the Duke may like this tribute to his humane exercise of the law), because the Duke is known to enjoy 'the sport' himself (ll. 100–5).

The Duke does not like to hear this and immediately objects (ll. 106–7). Lucio is too absorbed in his own banter to notice how sensitive his new friend is to taunts about the Duke. On the contrary, Lucio seizes on what he takes to be this friar's naiveté about the world to brag about his own connections. He boasts that he knows the Duke and, moreover, he knows why the Duke has left (ll. 114–15).

116–21 This is too extraordinary a claim for the Duke to let slip. He prompts for more, and Lucio disobliges him. He changes tack, suggesting that although most think the Duke wise, he is in fact completely the opposite. The Duke is taken aback at the suggestion that he might not be wise (l. 120). Lucio airily retorts that the Duke is a fool (l. 121). Lucio is a braggart and a show-off.

122–44 The Duke breaks his composure. This is too much. He may not have expected praise from Lucio, but this insult cuts deep. He overreacts (and Lucio may be startled to see the Duke become so hot). In the following exchange, the Duke badgers Lucio, who meekly protests that he *does* know the Duke well. The Duke is hardly listening and sternly warns Lucio that he will take the matter up with the Duke when he returns. To show he is serious, he demands to know Lucio's name (ll. 136–7). Lucio claims he is not afraid, but this is simply bravado (l. 140). The Duke does not believe him: ll. 141–3 are sarcastic, perhaps overly so. The Duke is in serious danger of forgetting his disguise.

145–58 Lucio has had enough of this, so he changes the subject. He has come to the prison for news of Claudio, hence his question to the Duke (l. 145). L. 146, the Duke's response, is puzzling since he already knows the answer. He may be being obstinate.

This prompts Lucio to return to the subject of the Duke. He speaks now at length and the Duke listens in silence. At first Lucio seems to backtrack as he looks forward to the Duke's return and again criticizes Angelo (ll. 147–52). Then, saying his farewell, he again calls into question the Duke's character (ll. 152–8). The whole speech reprises the points Lucio made to the Duke earlier. It is as if, having been temporarily bested by this outraged friar, Lucio now reasserts himself by quickly saying everything he has just said again. He leaves quickly, before the Duke can even say goodbye back to him. Lucio has the last word.

159–62   The Duke's world-weary soliloquy reflects on the injustices of being a good but unappreciated ruler. He is incredulous that Lucio should slander him so, yet hope for his return. He is stopped by a commotion.

163–76   As the Duke does not now speak for some time, he might withdraw to the back of the stage. Either he is looking to escape the approaching rabble, or he is interested to see Escalus among those leading Overdone and the rest. It is Escalus' voice that the Duke first hears when he registers the approaching posse. L. 163 is said by Escalus to the Provost and the officers. He sounds impatient. Mistress Overdone and the rest have been trying to get his attention as they enter.

In ll. 164–5, Mistress Overdone begs Escalus to help her. She is fawning and the lines can be very suggestive. It may be that Overdone is genuinely offering herself to Escalus as a bargain for her freedom, but she could just be teasing him. Escalus blusters a reply (ll. 166–7), and the Provost officiously tells him who Overdone is and how long she has been a prostitute (l. 168).

Mistress Overdone is not done over yet. Assuming that Lucio has informed on her, she angrily denounces him by revealing one of his shabby secrets, that he has a child out of marriage. This will interest the Duke, still watching quietly in the background (ll. 170–4). Escalus reflects that Lucio is indeed a liberal fellow and orders one of the officers to arrange for an interview (l. 175). He is not shocked; he sounds like a bureaucrat drowning under the paperwork for a new initiative.

Although she has no more lines, it will be out of character for Overdone not to carry on pleading and shouting as she is taken off to the cells, unless the officers find some way to silence her.

177–80   Escalus may wait until all the prisoners are gone. He can now speak candidly to the Provost about Claudio, although he has no consolation to offer him, except that he would not judge Claudio so harshly (Escalus does not seem to notice the Duke skulking in a dark corner). This is as much as he dare say and he is careful to call Angelo his brother. He sounds tired. The Provost does not ask him a question so this must be a matter that has been broached before the scene started.

181–98 The Provost brings the Duke over, introducing him to Escalus as Claudio's confessor. This is as much as he can do for Claudio.

The Duke may be a little reluctant to meet his adviser and will do all he can to hide his face. This is the first real test of his disguise. It is one thing to fool a subordinate, quite another to fool an old and trusted friend. Escalus, however, seems too defeated to take much notice. After a few brief questions the Duke, growing in confidence, risks speaking at some length about the troubles of the world. The sermon suits Escalus' gloomy mood and it seems designed to test the water. Now the Duke takes an even bigger risk by asking Escalus to tell him his thoughts about the Duke (ll. 191–8).

199–207 Escalus' reply is unintentionally ironic (l. 199). The Duke prods him further and now Escalus starts to speak freely. He has nothing but compliments for his master, which the Duke will enjoy hearing, but Escalus is not keen to talk at any length about this, and soon turns back to Claudio. He may feel uncomfortable about discussing his feelings about the Duke with a foreigner.

208–22 The Duke boasts that he has managed to ready Claudio for death (ll. 202–12). Escalus warms to this foreign friar and now tells him a little more than he should, that he has tried hard to save Claudio, that Angelo is too stern (ll. 213–17). The Duke's reply is deliberately prophetic (ll. 218–20), but Escalus does not comment. Instead he ends the conversation and exits to visit Claudio.

223–end of scene Alone and now able to execute his plan, the Duke ruminates on Angelo's hypocrisy and his own plan to defeat it. By moving from the verse-form to singing quatrains, Shakespeare signals a change of pace in the story. This soliloquy is urgent, angry, insistent. The first part (ll. 223–38) develops the point that the Duke (speaking as a friar) made to Escalus in ll. 218–20, only now he unburdens his real feelings about his Deputy.

He starts by describing the virtues of a good ruler (ll. 223–8), then talks specifically about Angelo (ll. 229–32). He takes Angelo's hypocrisy personally, contrasting his 'vice' (by which he means his failure to enforce the law) with Angelo's (l. 232). This is the Duke's most bitter line.

Perhaps after a pause, the Duke asks two questions to the air. What sort of world is it where men can be both angel and devil?

At l. 239, the Duke returns to his plot. It is this which gives him consolation and some sense of purpose. He enjoys the irony that Angelo will himself be deceived into virtue.

ACT IV

Act IV, scene i

1–22 The boy's song registers an important shift in location from the rough and ready world of prisons and brothels to one of the play's 'other places'. On a practical level, the boy's song gives the actor playing the Duke a brief time offstage, otherwise he enters almost as soon as leaves unless the interval is called after the end of Act III, scene ii.

Mariana interrupts the boy (l. 7) and hurries him offstage. She has seen the Duke approaching and she is embarrassed to be discovered enjoying herself. We learn that the Duke has often visited her in disguise; l. 22 affirms her longstanding relationship with the Duke's alter ego. The Duke sees Isabella coming and hastily asks Mariana to leave the stage.

23–4 The Duke is evidently glad to see Isabella, hence his effusive greeting. However, he is also keen to know whether Isabella went through with the plan and if Angelo took the bait. He is anxious and excited.

25–32 Isabella avoids answering the Duke's hasty question directly: instead she describes at some length Angelo's walled garden. She is hesitant, nervous and in no way as excited as the Duke is. She tells her story backwards, each line ending with an even rhythm, revealing a significant detail and building up in steady fragments to form a complete picture. It is only in the last lines that she tells the Duke what he is eager to hear.

33–46   The Duke is already beginning to fret, worried now that Isabella may not be able to carry out the plan. He presses Isabella (l. 34). She is embarrassed to tell him anything about her meeting with Angelo, which she evidently found humiliating. She tells the Duke about whispered instructions (ll. 34–7). He presses her again and now she is more revealing. Isabella has set terms that will make sure Marianna's chances of discovery are slim (ll. 39–43). This is more like the kind of news that the Duke was waiting for. However, he has himself been remiss, having sent Isabella to Angelo without first soliciting Marianna's help.

47–55   The Duke now summons Marianna and introduces her to Isabella. Although in charge, the Duke finds it necessary to test Marianna's trust in him again (l. 49). She will need some persuading but, before sending the two off for a private conference, the Duke reminds them to be quick. It is Marianna rather than Isabella who takes the lead; Marianna seems to be more confident, even though it is Isabella who has the story to tell (l. 55). Although talking silently, Isabella and Marianna remain onstage. The text offers no clues about this dumbshow, except that it will not take Isabella long to persuade Marianna to help her (alternatively, the two women could leave the stage briefly).

56–61   The audience will in any case be distracted by the Duke, who now has a short soliloquy. The dramatic purpose of this speech is simply to provide cover for Isabella and Marianna to talk without boring the audience with another recap of the plot. The story is moving faster now; there is no time for more exposition. The Duke briefly reflects on his own position as someone whom history will judge. It is a speech heavy with a sense of responsibility and the burden of duty.

62–4   Marianna is quickly persuaded and the pair return to the Duke. Anxious to know Marianna's reaction to Isabella's startling proposal, the Duke is brusque (l. 62). It is Isabella rather than Marianna who now replies. Having explained her purpose and secured a substitution for Angelo's bed, Isabella is less nervous than she was (ll. 63–4).

64–7   These lines are both addressed to Marianna who, although she says little, is now the centre of Isabella and the Duke's attention. Isabella impresses upon Marianna not to forget her brother in her meeting with Angelo.

68–end of scene   Marianna's three words at l. 68 show her to be resolute, but is she really unafraid? The Duke's short sermon is meant to be reassuring. The Duke leads Isabella and Marianna offstage, though both are uncertain about what will happen next.

Act IV, scene ii

1–14   The play returns to the prison and to the Provost, who is about to make a proposal to Pompey that is no less startling than the one Isabella made to Marianna (l. 1). This is a signal for the interlude of black comedy which dominates Act IV. The Provost is impatient with Pompey (perhaps he is annoyed that even his full punishment, a whipping and a term of imprisonment, is much less than Claudio's) (ll. 5–11). He is also preoccupied, as he will later have to give Claudio the warrant for his execution. Pompey is more than happy to escape punishment and readily agrees (ll. 12–14).

15–23   The Provost calls Abhorson onto the stage. Abhorson is a clownish executioner whose main concern is to protect the 'mystery' of his trade – perhaps a familiar protest from professionals in Shakespeare's audience (l. 22). He is offended to be given a pimp for an apprentice. However, as far as the Provost is concerned, there is not much difference between a bawd and an executioner (l. 23). He leaves the pair to discuss his proposal.

24–33   Left alone, Pompey and Abhorson start off somewhat awkwardly, since Abhorson is a reluctant master and he is suspicious of Pompey. The tapster tries to win his new employer over, though he cannot help commenting on Abhorson's gloomy look (ll. 24–6). However, Abhorson is difficult to draw, so Pompey tries again, this time using some absurd logic to see the mystery in prostitution, but baffled that there should be any secrets in hanging (ll. 28–31). Abhorson's reply is assertive but no more forthcoming, so Pompey demands that he prove his claim.

33–7   Abhorson's answers with a baffling treatise on the importance of making sure that the length of rope used for the hanging is just right. He speaks as if he were a tailor rather than an executioner, lovingly describing a trade secret. (Some editions ascribe these lines to Pompey.) It seems unlikely that Pompey will understand Abhorson, but he may enjoy listening to him all the same.

38–46   L. 38 is more an order than a question. Pompey replies as if he were a consumer rather than a prisoner. Yes, he will take the job, he says, as if he had given the question much thought, and then follows with an unlikely bit of reasoning (ll. 39–40). The Provost hardly listens, instead ordering Abhorson to bring his tools to the prison the next day.

In his own way, the morose hangman takes to his garrulous apprentice. He does not complain now about having a bawd learn his trade secrets. Instead, using as few words as he possibly can, he tells Pompey to come with him (l. 43). Pompey exaggerates an effusive reply. Abhorson must find it rare to be called kind, though he may scowl as the pair leave the stage (ll. 44–6).

47–9   L. 47 could be an instruction to Abhorson (on his way out), or the Provost could say it to an officer on or offstage. Having called for Barnadine and Claudio, the Provost reflects briefly on his two prisoners: he is sorry for Claudio, but he could never feel sorry for Barnadine (ll. 48–9).

50–2 The text's stage direction, 'Enter Claudio', is surely not sufficient. Convicts do not wander about their jails unescorted, so he
must be with officers, or at least in chains. The Provost has a job to do
that he finds difficult: he has to give Claudio the warrant for his
execution. He may have been holding the warrant for the whole
scene, or he may produce it now from a desk or a pocket. Either way,
the Provost has been dreading this moment since the scene began.
The Provost hides his emotions behind procedure and gives Claudio
the warrant in a professional, businesslike manner. However, there
may be a pause after his first word in l. 50, and both men will try to
gloss over the line's final word.

In l. 51 the Provost says that it is midnight. This is important infor-
mation for the story, as this is the time that Isabella set for her meeting with Angelo.

52–9 Claudio is alone, but the Provost expected to see two prisoners. The Provost questions Claudio about Barnadine who, we learn, is
still asleep. This little exchange, from the Provost's two-line soliloquy
(ll. 47–8) to Claudio's three lines (ll. 53–5), sets up audience expectations about this extraordinary-sounding character. Claudio's speech
is his last in the play and soon after he exits without another word. As
he does so, a furious knocking starts.

The Provost shouts that he is coming (l. 57) and then mutters to
himself that he hopes for news of a pardon (ll. 58–9). When he greets
the Duke, he does so with a little disappointment.

60–5 The Duke, however, is in a cheerful mood. In ll. 60–1, he
surprises the Provost with an upbeat hello and a leading question:
who has visited the prison? Puzzled, the Provost says that no one has
come. Now the Duke is concerned. Not even Isabella? The Duke is
momentarily dumbfounded when the Provost says no, but he
quickly recovers himself. He's just early; these things do not always
go according to plan. She will be along soon (l. 63).

The Provost evidently realizes that the Duke knows more than he
is telling and pointedly asks what good this will do Claudio. The
Duke is confident enough to broadly hint that the Provost is right to
think there may be hope after all (l. 65).

65–72   A pause is implied between the Duke's part of l. 65 and the Provost's, as the Provost now changes the topic to that of the Deputy. This is the strongest language we have yet heard from the Provost.

As he is utterly confident in his own scheme, the Duke takes umbrage at the Provost's dig at Angelo, whom he now eloquently defends. Angelo may be a stern Deputy but he is able to master his own passions, says the Duke, confident enough to lie. Claudio must be saved, but justice must not be questioned.

72–6   The Duke is interrupted by more knocking, which takes the Provost offstage. He assumes that Isabella and Marianna have arrived, or a pardon has been sent (l. 72). However, he is anxious and excited enough to switch moods quickly. He first reflects on the Provost's good qualities (ll. 73–4), but when the knocking continues, he suddenly becomes short-tempered (ll. 75–6).

77–88   The Provost is talking to someone offstage, giving them instructions about Claudio (ll. 77–8). The Duke, who has been waiting anxiously for news, immediately seizes upon this as a sign that Claudio has not been pardoned (ll. 79–80). The Provost has had no word from Angelo, but the Duke decides to remain optimistic, though he is beginning to have his doubts; he sounds as though he is trying to reassure himself (ll. 81–2).

The Duke has dropped more than enough hints now that he has good reason to expect a pardon. However, the Provost is unconvinced. Whatever it is that the Duke knows, the Provost does not believe a pardon will come because Angelo has staked too much on this execution as proof of his authority (ll. 82–7). The Provost is more of a realist than the Duke. At that moment, the Provost spots Angelo's servant arriving on the stage. Confident that the Provost is wrong, the Duke boasts that the messenger brings a pardon (perhaps spotting a letter in his hand).

89–93   The messenger is brief but insistent. The note he gives the Provost is evidently important. The Duke watches the Provost take the note with excited interest. The Provost is more dour (l. 93).

94–100   This short soliloquy (which is probably an aside) is said by the Duke as he watches the Provost read the note. The Duke's anticipation will not match the Provost, who will read the note with resignation. The Duke is in a self-congratulatory mood, but he cannot help reflect on the irony that Angelo and Claudio have committed the same offence. Either the Provost starts putting the note away or the Duke thinks it odd not to see some better reaction from him, as the Duke now has to prompt him (l. 100).

101–11   The Provost is right: Angelo is not about to pardon Claudio. However, the Provost is puzzled. Why is Angelo reminding him to execute Claudio, why does he insist on seeing Claudio's head? The Provost thinks Angelo is questioning his abilities. At the Duke's prompting, he reads the letter out loud. Maybe this friar can shed some light on this strange communication?

112–34   Matters are now urgent and the Duke has to think fast. As soon as the Provost has finished reading Angelo's order, the Duke considers switching Barnadine and Claudio. He is thinking on his feet. There is something comic about the way the Duke switches tack, and something pathetic about his refusal to do what he always could do and step out of his disguise to remedy the situation.

How does the Duke react when the speech is read, and how quickly does he respond? A pause seems warranted after the message: a short pause will be funny, a longer pause will bring out the seriousness of the situation. The Duke does not even answer the Provost's question, instead he asks a question of his own and the audience (and perhaps the Provost) may already be beginning to guess what he has in mind. The little exchange that follows not only shows the Duke interrogating the Provost and sounding less and less like a friar (does the Provost react to this change of character? Does he suspect?), it also introduces us to Barnadine.

135–44   The Duke's next speech is full of words which indicate his anxious, fast-thinking state of mind: 'boldness', 'dangerous', 'cunning', 'hazard'. He flatters the Provost but his description is probably a good indication for the actor playing that part to work with:

'honesty' and 'constancy'. The Duke's new plan is almost identical to his last, only this time the body to be switched is not that of a young virgin but of an executed criminal. And once again, the Duke has to solicit trust – but this time he has to break cover.

145–end of scene   The Provost blathers when he hears the Duke's proposal and falls back on the administrative difficulties of pulling the scheme off. He is difficult to persuade, especially as the Duke's plan sounds increasingly bizarre and outlandish. Perhaps recovering from his initial surprise, the Provost offers a more blunt response (l. 159). The Duke is forced to reveal a little of his hand. The Provost must be almost as surprised as he was before when he sees the Duke's seal – does he suspect? The Provost leaves with the Duke without another word. Friar or not, the Duke is issuing orders now.

Act IV, scene iii

There is a quickening of the pace as events rush towards the denouement. The debates of the middle section of the play are over. The Duke is hastily stage-managing his return, characters enter and leave quickly. The Duke is now the centre of the play. The audience might expect now to track Isabella and Claudio's story, but tension here is eased because we already know that Claudio has been saved. The question now, which creates suspense and expectation, is how will the Duke resolve matters? And why does he lie to Isabella in this scene, which to modern (and probably early modern) ears, is cruel?

1–16   Pompey is enjoying his new job as executioner's apprentice. As a pimp-turned-executioner, he even draws attention to the similarity between the prison and his whorehouse (l. 2). This is said as consolation: after all, both cell and brothel are places where social orders criss-cross. He develops the joke – many of his former customers are waiting for him.

Pompey now addresses a number of these inmates directly. There is no reason why he should not be talking to those onstage, but the soliloquy is meant to be played to the audience as if *they* were

Pompey's old and new customers. This speech lends itself well to improvisation and audience interaction.

17–25 Abhorson enters, interrupting Pompey's monologue with a curt order to fetch Barnadine. Both now shout Barnadine's name loudly and make a commotion to wake him up. Barnadine shouts back insults from offstage. He is too tired to be hanged (l. 25).

26–32 Pompey and Abhorson are apprehensive. As the master, Abhorson decides to give his apprentice the job of waking Barnadine up but Pompey is reluctant to go into Barnadine's cell. Neither has the courage to face him. Pompey insists that he can hear Barnadine coming, so there's no need to go in and get him (l. 30). As soon as he sees Barnadine, Abhorson checks with Pompey that the executioner's block is ready: he wants things done as speedily as possible.

33–40 Barnadine must be frightening. With just one apparently polite question (l. 33), he has the taciturn Abhorson talking with excessive deference. Barnadine bites back that he has a hangover (ll. 36–7). Abhorson probably quakes; Pompey cannot resist a quip about hanging being the best cure for a hangover (l. 40).

41–54 Fortunately for Pompey and Abhorson, the Duke enters and Abhorson uses the opportunity to deflect Barnadine's hot-tempered attention. However, the Duke's entrance does not help matters, in fact he proves to be as ineffectual as the hapless executioners. His initial haste offends Barnadine. L. 49 sounds more like a plea than a command. Barnadine retreats back to his cell, infuriatingly stubborn, and the axe and its block remain unused.

55–9 Perhaps forgetting for a moment that he is a friar, the Duke sends the executioners after Barnadine. He is watched by the Provost, who has just entered. The Provost may have suspected all along that Barnadine would not be so easy to substitute for Claudio. Fortunately, he has another idea to suggest to the Duke, who appears to be at his wit's end (ll. 58–9).

60–83　Despite all his reservations, the Provost has decided to help the Duke and Claudio. The Duke is delighted and eagerly accepts the Provost's proposal to use Ragozine's head in place of Barnadine's. In return, the Duke promises to persuade Barnadine to come to his death willingly (this is a promise that he does not keep).

Now that the Provost has stepped outside the law, he has become the Duke's confederate, and in l. 82 he acknowledges that his future is now in this foreign friar's hands.

84–92　The Duke speaks quickly, improvising plans. He must be writing the letters as he speaks, as he intends to give them to the Provost to deliver along with Ragozine's head. It is important to know at this point how far the Duke has planned for this moment. He could have been intending to expose Angelo in a public show from the beginning, in which case all he does here is slightly alter his scheme. However, it is also possible to read the speech as if the Duke is developing his plan as he goes along: I'll write to Angelo to tell him I'm coming home, why not make my return public? (l. 88). At l. 90, his tone suddenly becomes more serious as he reflects on what he will do with Angelo when he confronts him. At l. 92, the speech slows darkly. 'Proceed' is a euphemism – but what *will* the Duke do with Angelo?

93–6　The Duke is interrupted by the Provost who returns (probably out of breath) with Ragozine's head ready to be taken to Angelo. The Duke must at this point give the Provost the letter that he has just written. In l. 93, the Provost states the obvious (it is difficult to conceal a head). The Duke's tone has become serious and he is brief with the Provost (ll. 94–6).

97–114　Isabella calls offstage, interrupting the Duke. Still thinking on his feet, he decides to tell her that Claudio is dead. In trying to be a friar, the Duke is amusingly tactless. Isabella brushes off his first sunny greeting; she is impatient for news (ll. 104–6); the Duke tells her bluntly that Claudio is dead (ll. 107–8). She cries (the Duke tells her to dry her eyes at l. 119), but she is also angry and threatens to immediately confront (and attack) Angelo.

The Duke may wonder if another of his plans has backfired. It is vital that he keep Isabella from Angelo until the proper time, so he restrains her. L. 112 is ambiguous: the Duke says that Isabella will not be allowed to see Angelo but he also means that she should not go, at least not like this. Isabella is out of control; the Duke needs to be assertive.

115–40   In this long speech (punctured only once by Isabella at l. 128), the Duke calms Isabella down, convinces her to trust him, and readies her for the final act. He begins by telling her that she will neither hurt Angelo nor help herself by acting rashly (l. 115). He tries to talk tenderly but Isabella is still wild with emotion and, it seems, hardly listening, as he has to tell her at l. 119 to stop crying. He persuades her now to appeal to the Duke in public.

Ll. 129–35 are straightforward. The Duke gives Isabella a letter (did he write this one onstage as well?) and gives her instructions. In the second part of l. 135, the Duke takes a risk and makes up an excuse to explain why he cannot go with her.

141–8   Lucio enters, looking for the Provost. He greets both Isabella and the Duke, and then rudely asks the Duke where the Provost is. Annoyed, the Duke forces himself to reply (ll. 141–2). He is tactless and risks being distracted by his irritation with Lucio who is, for once, in a grave mood.

Lucio may be a rogue and a man-about-town, but he is tender with Isabella, whom he comforts almost as if she was his sister. The Duke is too involved in his schemes, too anxious about keeping all the elements of his plan going, to note the devastating impact of Claudio's supposed death on the woman to whom he will later propose.

149–end of scene   As Isabella leaves the stage, the Duke is fuming. Once again, he decides to chide Lucio for talking about the returning Duke in such a derogatory way. This exchange is a reprise of Lucio and the Duke's first meeting. At l. 153, the Duke, remembering that he will soon be able to deal with Lucio, tries to end their conversation with a brief warning. But Lucio will not let go. He has many more stories about the Duke, he brags, and is determined to tell them.

Now Lucio makes a mistake by boasting that he was once taken before the Duke for getting a woman pregnant (l. 158). Evidently he then denied it, but he privately admits to the Duke now that he was guilty after all. The Duke is glad to know this and more content to say goodbye to Lucio, who is proving difficult to shake off (l. 165).

Act IV, scene iv

Several short scenes now follow, the shortest in the play, which build up pace and tension.

1–17   Angelo and Escalus puzzle over the Duke's letters; Escalus is simply baffled (l. 1). Angelo is unsettled by the Duke's behaviour and worries at length about what it means (ll. 2–5). Their reactions contrast. Although puzzled, Escalus does not want to speculate too much about the Duke's questions (l. 6). Angelo is agitated and less in control than he was (ll. 7–9). He reluctantly gives the order to announce the Duke's return (ll. 13–15).

Although he says nothing, Escalus may notice how distracted the usually surefooted Angelo is.

18–end of scene   Alone, Angelo starts to fall apart. This speech shows his moral confusion as he attempts to justify his actions. He detaches himself from his crime by talking about himself in the third person (l. 20). He justifies Claudio's execution not on the grounds of Claudio's guilt but on the much more selfish argument that Claudio would have taken his revenge if he had lived (ll. 26–30). Angelo's thoughts dwell on self-preservation, but he is also still able to articulate the moral conflict between law and desire. By the end of the speech, Angelo is apparently lost (l. 32).

Act IV, scene v

1–end of scene   The Duke is no longer dressed as a friar and he presses letters into Friar Peter's hands with evident urgency. His orders are uncharacteristically concise.

The scene presents a couple of narrative oddities about which

there has been much textual argument. Yet the scene does work
theatrically: the Duke's torrent of names suggests hustle and bustle.
The scene reminds us that the Duke has hastily put his plans together
and needs to act fast with people he can trust to make his scheme
work.

Act IV, scene vi

Although the last three scenes of Act IV all point to Act V, there may
be a short pause between scenes v and vi. Scenes iv and v go together;
they both show the build up to the Duke's return. However, now
some time has passed and Act V is about to begin – this scene is in
fact a prologue to Act V and leads straight into it (l. 15).

1–end of scene Isabella and Marianna are getting ready for the
Duke's return, nervous because the Friar isn't there, curious about
some of his instructions, and finding resolve to face Angelo. Isabella
is struggling with her anger; she says in l. 1 that she does not want to
say out loud what she is thinking. She wants to tell the truth, but
steels herself to speak as if it were she who slept with Angelo.
Marianna is quite insistent that they follow the Friar's orders (l. 4).
Then we have a curious plot detail, which may explain some of
Isabella's doubts – the Friar may speak against them (l. 6). Marianna
is anxious for Friar Peter to come (presumably, she is about to say, 'I
wish Friar Peter would hurry up'). When he does arrive, he quickly
hurries them off the stage.

ACT V

Act V, scene i

The last scene of the play comprises several different episodes all
played out in the same location. The Duke must be both judge and
witness without revealing himself until exactly the right moment. Such
costume gymnastics are more typical of farce, but the scene is not
comedic: played right, it is full of suspense and unsettling revelations.

We know what the Duke has to do but we do not know the method. We already understand what will happen: we know that Claudio is alive, that Isabella is still a virgin, that Angelo has been rumbled. There are no surprises, no last-minute twists (save the Duke's proposal to Isabella, more of which later).

1–18   The opening is grand. Despite the Duke's convivial tone, the actors should treat the situation as formal. Angelo bows deferentially at the front of his delegation (the rest bowing too). Angelo is not sincere when he greets the Duke but his fears are buried deep (l. 3).

The Duke is not going to let Angelo get away with this so, aware of Angelo's inner discomfort, the Duke deliberately emphasizes Angelo's good works and admonishes him for his false modesty (ll. 4–8). Angelo squirms a little (l. 9) but the Duke continues to flatter him (ll. 9–16). By this point the Duke has released Angelo from his vow and may be embracing him, clapping his shoulders, etc., to make Angelo even more uncomfortable. When the Duke asks for his Deputy's hand (l. 13), Angelo will give it, but reluctantly. The Duke then calls Escalus to his other hand.

19–25   Friar Peter now pushes Isabella to face the Duke. That Isabella does not know that the Duke is the true author, the real stage manager, of everything she has done since meeting the Friar, gives this scene a peculiar energy. There is no risk for the Duke, but Isabella risks everything. Her appeal will make an accusation against the Duke's deputy, his favourite. She is going to upset the order of things at the very moment that the Duke is celebrating his resumption of power. And because Isabella is not at this point going to reveal Marianna's role in the story, she is also risking her honour, the very thing that she has fought so hard to guard ever since we first saw her retreating from the world to a convent. The Duke gambles nothing, but for Isabella everything is risk and all she has to secure herself is her trust in a friar who she hardly knows and who has not come to help her.

L. 19 is a heavy line, now *is* the time to 'speak loud'. Isabella, who begins and ends the play in silence, and who earlier demanded 'to whom should I complain', now has her moment.

The Friar tells us how the part is played: Isabella kneels and she speaks loud, both literally and in her subject matter. She interrupts the Duke, who has not solicited her suit yet but is, we know from his last speech, walking about his subjects with his deputies on either side of him. Isabella forcefully reverses this relationship between sovereign and subject with one word, one demand: 'Justice' (l. 20). Does even the Duke expect such force from Isabella? With that one loud word, Isabella changes everything: now the sovereign sees *her*, now he will *know*.

26–32 The Duke is startled, he answers abruptly, he questions, he defers to Angelo (l. 28). How much of this is an act, how much is the Duke genuinely taken aback by the strength of Isabella's complaint?

Isabella again demands the Duke's attention (ll. 28–32). The Duke is being given very little choice but to listen. It must be him and not Angelo who hears her complaint.

33–6 Angelo keeps himself measured: ignore her, she is mad. Look at the way she complains, he says, she is just upset, her brother met his punishment (ll. 33–4). Both terrified and angry, he readies himself to destroy Isabella. He has no choice, even though this is far beyond what he ever intended, or thought himself capable of. When Isabella mocks his references to justice (l. 35), Angelo starts to discredit her: she will say strange things, he promises (l. 36).

37–46 Reminding us how adept she is at debating, Isabella takes Angelo's words and throws them back at him. Strange, yes, but the truth is sometimes strange (l. 37). She uses harsh words, the harshest she can, against Angelo – he is a murderer, a thief, and so on. She lashes out, furious that Angelo should call her mad. And she pummels both Angelo and the Duke without any of the dutiful respect she showed in her first scene, but with pure anger. The Duke pretends to be baffled (l. 43), but Isabella continues her tirade.

46–7 Appearing to trust his deputy, the Duke orders Isabella away because she is deranged. The Duke is testing Isabella by making it so difficult for her, but he is also testing Angelo, who is now under pressure to confess. How far will Angelo go? Is he prepared to destroy Isabella?

48–59   Isabella realizes she has gone too far. No one comes to take her away: perhaps the guards are wary of her, or maybe she shrugs them off. She speaks now with restraint, appealing directly to the Duke, begging not to be dismissed as a madwoman. With calm conviction and strong words, she accuses Angelo of hypocrisy.

59–68   The Duke continues to pretend to believe Isabella is mad but, perhaps to Angelo's surprise, he now loudly wonders what kind of madness it must be that seems to speak so much sense. The Duke is playing games, provoking Isabella and worrying Angelo at the same time. Frustrated, Isabella urges the Duke not to dwell on the question of her sanity but to listen to her complaint (ll. 63–7). Feigning amused indifference, the Duke offers to hear her, but it must seem to Isabella that the Duke is not very interested.

69–91   Isabella draws her breath and then starts to make her accusation. Her speech sounds rehearsed and she has to talk loudly and with confidence to rise above the noise of the startled crowd around her. However, things do not go smoothly. Hearing his name, Lucio interrupts her and the Duke, as irritated as he always is by Lucio, rudely argues with him (ll. 78–85). The Duke gives something small away here, his irritation with Lucio at odds with his feigned indifference to Isabella's suit. Lucio is cocky and defiant – he wasn't asked to speak, he wasn't asked to be quiet either. When this fracas is over, Isabella starts again, but this time the Duke interrupts her by questioning her description of Angelo. Perhaps she is mad after all?

92–103   Now given the floor, Isabella tells her story with vivid and compelling words, capturing in language her exchanges with Angelo. Angelo was vile, she full of grief and shame. This is a powerful speech, its words artfully directed with controlled passion. And they pile on: with l. 98 Isabella effectively says the same thing thrice, hammering the point but with formal language rather than hasty accusations.

103–14   The Duke, feigning shock, accuses her again of being mad or deceitful. What he does not do, which we might expect of him, is ask Angelo for a response. Instead, the Duke praises his deputy's virtue and presses Isabella to reveal who has put her up to this. The Duke's strategy is to create a situation where his alter ego will be brought onstage and he is manipulating the conversation to achieve this, at the same time making Angelo even more uncomfortable.

114–23   Frustrated, Isabella gives up. Just as she did with Angelo in her first meeting, Isabella speaks as if she is about to walk away, disappointed and resigned (l. 114). Is that all justice is capable of? Is the Duke really that impotent? Is she that alone? She makes a brief prayer, no longer confident in the Duke's authority to dispense justice – and creating a minor problem for the Duke, who needs to keep Isabella onstage if his plans are to continue. The Duke rescues the situation by arresting her, but things are getting out of control (ll. 120–1).

124–36   Guards restrain Isabella and the Duke becomes an interrogator – who sent you, who put you up to this? Isabella names the Duke's alter ego and the Duke mocks her in return. 'A ghostly father' might even be a sexual sneer. Who knows Lodowick? Naturally, Lucio makes his answer, this time able to speak without censure. Again, not knowing that the Duke is the Friar, Lucio outrageously slanders him to the Duke's face (l. 136).

137–62   The other friar, Peter, now speaks at length. Until now, there has been confusion and outrage on the stage. In this long speech, Peter coolly promises that he can settle the questions Isabella has raised. He seems to side with the Duke and Angelo but this is, of course, pretence. He and the Duke have rehearsed this bit of the scene already. The Duke's intention is to increase the pressure on Angelo.

Isabella is now silenced. Friar Peter has discredited her story. Glad that events seem to be moving in his favour, Angelo experiences a moment of false security, or perhaps a slight unease. After all, who is this friar with proof of his innocence, when Angelo is anything but innocent? Friar Peter is one of those small parts with an important role. He is both messenger and intermediary; without him the play cannot happen yet, like Isabella, like the Duke, he has to mislead to reveal the truth.

163–7 With Isabella gone, the Duke changes his strategy. Now he treats the whole situation as a bit of a (cruel) joke. In l. 163, the Duke encourages Angelo to see the humour in this apparently ridiculous situation. The more he talks Angelo up, the more Angelo has to lose – both know this. To further Angelo's embarrassment, the Duke calls for chairs to be brought on to the stage (l. 165). The entrance party has now been reassembled as a court. Mischievously, the Duke makes Angelo the judge in his own trial (ll. 166–7).

167–77 Peter brings Marianna onto the stage to stand, veiled, before the court. Feigning curiosity, the Duke demands that she show her face but Marianna refuses to lift her veil: like Isabella, she is not easily commanded (ll. 167–70).

Marianna hides more than just her face. Her answers to the Duke's initial questions make her even more mysterious. In contrast to Isabella, Marianna controls herself and commands the scene. She sets what seems to be an impossible rule: she will only show her face to her husband. What is she if she is not a maid, a wife or a widow (ll. 171–7)?

178–82 Lucio has got it: she must be a prostitute. His joke is a reminder of the culture of female dispossession with which the play concerns itself. The Duke abruptly tells him to shut up (l. 180).

183–90 Mariana continues with her riddles. She has slept with her husband without her husband's knowledge (ll. 183–6). Lucio has an answer to this riddle as well: the husband was drunk. Again, Lucio (speaking more like Pompey) reduces the scene to sexual debauchery and the Duke is dismissive (ll. 187–8).

The riddle seems irrelevant to the accusations against Angelo, and others in the court may wonder why the Duke does not simply dismiss the case (l. 190).

191–201   Marianna's answer adds to the confusion, as she claims that Isabella has also made accusations against her husband (ll. 191–6). Angelo is puzzled: surely there cannot be other men that she has slept with (l. 197)? Prompted by the Duke, Mariana now claims that Angelo is her husband.

202–3   Angry, Angelo insists she take off her veil (l. 202). He needs to see who she is; perhaps he is already beginning to suspect. But surely this woman can't be Marianna, after all this time?

Marianna willingly lifts her veil to show her face. This is a powerful moment for Marianna and a devastating one for Angelo. He was ready to face Isabella's accusations and bury his guilt, but he is unprepared to see Marianna. In a resolute voice, she calls him her husband.

204–10   Angelo does not speak. Having got his attention, Marianna speaks firmly, pointing out to him different parts of her body, the body which *he* owns. This is the body, she says, that Angelo took during the night. Marianna presents herself to Angelo as an object but she does so scornfully: this is the thing cruel Angelo has both denied and possessed.

The Duke asks Angelo a direct question; perhaps he is still not taking these claims seriously, but this brief line suggests he is (pretending to) lose his patience. Marianna stands quietly, waiting for Angelo's response. Is Angelo fascinated, horrified; does he even avoid looking at her?

211–13   Lucio, preoccupied as ever with crudity, interrupts. The Duke, with less patience than before, cuts him off. Realizing he has gone too far, Lucio backs down.

214–22   The delay gives Angelo a few seconds to compose his answer, to think through his strategy. He first rubbishes Marianna – yes, there was some vague talk of getting married but her dowry was not what I wanted and more than that (something not mentioned by the Duke before) there were questions about her 'reputation'. People made jokes about her, I have not seen her since, these are strange accusations.

222–37   Marianna, who is evidently still kneeling (as she threatens to stay that way and become a statue), develops her point, insists she is Angelo's wife and gives a more detailed account of the bed-trick (ll. 222–31). She addresses the Duke directly, but it is Angelo, who is after all judge of his own complaint, who responds.

Angelo readies himself to make a firm refutation of the claims made against *his* reputation. He has no way to answer these claims; his best tack is to blame someone else. Someone set them up, he is being framed, there is a darker force at work (ll. 231–7). He is falling for the Duke's trap; everything now points to the Duke's alter ego's role in the story.

237–52   The Duke feigns indifference, impatience even. By speaking dismissively of Isabella (l. 240), he casually denies her an identity. He talks as if he is not taking her story, nor that of the 'foolish friar' and 'pernicious woman' Marianna, seriously at all (l. 239). Wearily, he demands that the other friar be sent for – which sets up an interesting narrative problem, how will the Duke take on his alter ego without giving himself away?

253–7   The Duke has to find a way off the stage. He has summoned the Friar; the whole plot will fall apart if he doesn't leave now and there is still much to be revealed. But his departure must strike his subjects as odd; they have all gathered to see his return, not to see him once again entrust his authority to his Deputy. The Duke offers no convincing reason for his exit, he just goes (much as Angelo did when judging Froth's case). Escalus takes over; Angelo remains silent as if he too abrogates responsibility.

257–68   In a manner which recalls and mirrors his interrogation of Elbow and Pompey, Escalus turns to Lucio, the one man to whom the Duke would not listen. Lucio shows off with a pompous Latin quotation and then outrageously accuses the Friar of saying things that he himself said (ll. 260–3). Escalus recalls Isabella to the stage – the scenario for the denouement is gradually being composed (ll. 267–8).

269–83   Escalus and Lucio make an unlikely double act, but Lucio looks like he knows what he is talking about and, with the Duke gone and Angelo silent, Escalus keeps turning to him for support. Escalus boasts that he can interrogate Isabella and, surprisingly, Angelo appears to let him, for he says nothing in reply (ll. 269–70).

Angelo is not the only silent figure onstage – Marianna too says nothing, yet there is much that needs to be said, and may be said without words, between the two of them.

Through association with Lucio, Escalus cuts a slightly ridiculous figure as he attempts to judge the situation. Lucio makes a joke of Escalus' choice of language – he will handle her better than Angelo all right, but best do it in private (l. 271). The Duke would have hotly shouted Lucio down, but neither Angelo nor Escalus censure him. Perhaps they do not get the joke.

Isabella is brought back onstage, the Duke (in disguise) skulking behind her. Escalus begins to question Isabella but Lucio interrupts to point out the Duke/Friar (l. 279). At last, Escalus tells Lucio to be silent and Lucio, either surprised or amused, shuts his mouth (l. 283). Escalus ignores Isabella: it is now the Friar who will be questioned.

284–99   The Friar is a slippery subject, not easily bowed by authority, making impossible demands to see the Duke, robbing those there of authority over him (ll. 288–90). But Escalus is assertive, although in the context of the play, his take on political theory may have bawdy connotations (l. 291). Lucio patiently resists a comment. The Friar, more eloquent than he ever was as the Duke, speaks boldly. He commands the stage, he refuses to answer the charges put to him and instead argues that it is absurd for Angelo to judge an accusation made against his own person (ll. 292–9).

300–19   Lucio sees things differently – the Friar is busy living up to the reputation Lucio slanderously invented for him. L. 300 is a triumphant boast. Escalus is stern, perhaps too stern. We see his limits as a judge. He does not ask questions, but excoriates the Friar, threatens him with torture and scorns his religious authority. He casts the Friar as a manipulator (which he is of course) and a slanderer (ll. 301–9).

It is strange that neither Isabella nor Marianna say anything. Either they know their place, or the Duke gestures to them to be silent.

Now the Duke tries to calm things down (l. 309). He styles himself as an outsider, an observer. Speaking as a friar, the Duke condemns Vienna's corruption and accuses Angelo of mocking the law (ll. 309–18). Escalus has had enough; this Friar has gone too far and must go to jail (ll. 318–19). And still Angelo is silent – but now he gets to speak.

320–42   However, Angelo speaks to Lucio, the only character who both knows the Duke/Friar and accuses him (ll. 320–1). Lucio becomes prosecuting counsel, probes the Friar about their meeting but fails to rattle him; instead, the Duke turns the tables on Lucio, accuses Lucio of traducing the Duke, and so on. Lucio is being set up (ll. 320–35).

The Duke has an opportunity now to bring the scene back to his purpose. Like Marianna, he also speaks in riddles, and boasts that he loves the Duke as much as he does himself (l. 336). Angelo laughs – surely this friar is just trying to wriggle out of a treason charge (l. 337)? Escalus has lost all patience. He orders that all three, the Friar, Isabella and Marianna, should be taken to prison (ll. 339–42).

343–9   At Escalus' order, the Provost moves to restrain the Duke, who resists. Frustrated, Angelo sends Lucio to help the Provost (ll. 343–4). There is a commotion which ends when Lucio pulls the Friar's hood down and discovers the Duke. There will be a pause, a moment for shock and reaction. The Duke is finally exposed and the reaction is electric: a stunned court, a worried Lucio, a guilt-ridden Angelo. Even Isabella and Marianna are surprised. Feeling confident, the Duke even manages a joke at Lucio's expense (l. 349).

350–67   In command now, the Duke has the Provost release the women and arrest Lucio who, it seems, is trying to sneak away, sensing the game is up (ll. 351–2). So does Angelo, but for him the matter is more serious. The Duke does not need to explain anything, Angelo knows that the whole story will now come out and he will be ruined. The Duke threatens to tell his tale, but Angelo silences him with a moving confession and a plea for immediate death (ll. 359–67).

368–72   Ignoring Angelo for the moment, the Duke gently asks Marianna to come to him and then, more sternly, faces Angelo and demands to know if he is betrothed to her. Angelo has no choice but to say yes. The Duke may linger a moment before l. 370, to consider how best to punish Angelo and reward Marianna. He sends them off to be married and with the Provost and Friar Peter accompanying them, the stage is suddenly less crowded.

373–80   Escalus, who has been watching Angelo's fall in silence, briefly comments on it, but he is ignored. Instead, the Duke turns to Isabella and tenderly puts himself at her service. Isabella asks for pardon. This seems strange to modern ears, since the Duke has deceived her (and continues to deceive her). Yet her words here have more emotion in them than simple duty. Isabella means it when she apologizes for having 'pained' the Duke's sovereignty (l. 380).

380–92   The Duke is still performing a part, however. He now asks Isabella to pardon him for not being able to save Claudio, when he could at any time have revealed his power and used it (ll. 384–6). He argues (rather weakly) that Claudio's death came too quickly for him to act and then, sounding more like a friar again, endeavours to persuade Isabella that Claudio is better for being dead. Isabella gladly takes this consolation (l. 392).

393–409   The Duke turns from talking to Isabella to address Angelo, who is coming back onto the stage with Marianna, the pair now married. He speaks to Isabella but his remarks are meant for Angelo as well. In l. 393, the Duke mocks his Deputy but reminds Isabella that she has protected her honour (l. 395). This speech is a crucial one, not least because in hammering out the moral of the story, the Duke quotes the play's title (l. 404). He talks about mercy in stern terms. Mercy means an eye for an eye, measure for measure, an Angelo for a Claudio. He was tender with Isabella before, but he now grows serious and acts as one determined not to repeat the mistake that led to Claudio's death (this is of course an act). By refusing to address Angelo directly, the Duke shows his contempt for his former Deputy. Angelo's fate is settled; as the Duke points out, Angelo himself called for such a punishment. His speech builds to the moment where the order is issued for Angelo's execution (ll. 405–9).

409–22   The assembled crowd's reaction might be more mixed: Marianna especially is shocked. The Duke had appeared to be merciful when ordering that they be married; now Marianna has to plead for her husband, which she does immediately (ll. 409–10). She is spontaneous, more direct and cutting than she should be to her sovereign.

The Duke may notice this affront, for he uses Marianna's own words back at her, as if angry at her presumption (l. 411). He is curt and dismissive – Marianna should be happy with what she's got, although what she has is not much more than what she started with (ll. 412–18). Beaten back but still desperate, Marianna tries to plead with the Duke, but he is firm and orders that Angelo be sent away (ll. 418–20). She kneels, but he ignores her and shows his contempt for Angelo by talking to Lucio.

423–36   The Duke is manipulating the situation by putting pressure on Isabella: only Isabella can save Angelo. So sharp is he that Marianna is forced to plead to Isabella, who is now her last hope (ll. 423–5).

What happens to Angelo here is not clear and is something to work through – there is no easy answer; at some point the soldiers charged with taking him away must stop, or be stopped, but there is no obvious place for this to happen. At the very least, the dialogue should be fast and explosive: Marianna is desperate, the Duke feigns anger and darkly insists that Angelo must die (l. 436).

437–47   Then, in an extraordinary twist, Isabella kneels beside Marianna. The symbolic power of Isabella kneeling to the Duke drives the scene. As the Duke and Marianna shout at each other, as Marianna pleads to Isabella, the real scene will be played in silence by Isabella, who does not immediately respond to Marianna's request, who may look first at Angelo, may remember her brother, before finally kneeling.

Although Marianna did not ask for Isabella's voice, she speaks anyway. She not only pleads for Angelo's life but also challenges the Duke's authority and judgement. She concludes that intents and thoughts are not subjects, are free from the Duke's authority. Given that so much of the play is about the regulation of desire and the exposure of hidden thoughts, this is a potent speech. Isabella is restrained; she does not plead for Angelo, but she does persuade. She speaks like a defence counsel, only partly recalling her earlier supplications to Angelo (ll. 437–47).

The full stop in l. 439 opens up space for doubt and hesitation: he was OK until he looked at me, perhaps it was my fault? The next line is quick, said almost with embarrassment. The rest is difficult to say, but it is the truth and everyone onstage knows it is. As Isabella argues beautifully but with modesty that thoughts are not subjects, what is inside should remain free, she also speaks her last lines in the play. From now on, she has only thoughts.

447–51 Marianna stresses one of Isabella's words. Intents are not just thoughts, they are *merely* thoughts and not worth executing someone for (l. 448). Marianna shows her mettle here; she is brave to be so insistent to the Duke. She is, of course, still kneeling as the Duke commands her to stand; there is perhaps opportunity for a pause here, as the Duke suddenly changes tack. He is not ready to pardon Angelo yet and Isabella's eloquent plea seems to have caught him off guard. He now asks the Provost about Claudio's death.

451–62 The Provost already knows about the Claudio–Ragozine switch and must now pretend to be sacked – if the Duke is pretending (the Provost may have his doubts). But dutiful and trusting, the Provost goes along with the deception and his worry, his penitence, is an act. There is a gap after the semicolon in l. 453. Having thrown himself on the Duke's mercy, the Provost now thinks (or pretends to think) of mitigation: 'I knew I did wrong so I didn't execute Barnadine' (perhaps this is something the Provost has already rehearsed with the Duke). The Duke continues the charade; he is grave and sincere when speaking of Claudio, impatient when sending the Provost to fetch Barnadine. The Provost hurries offstage without saying another word (ll. 460–2).

463–70   The little exchange between Escalus and Angelo is a digression said privately between them. It gives space for Claudio to be plausibly fetched onstage from the prison (one way to play this is an awkward silence which Escalus breaks). Escalus is in earnest – to Angelo's face he says 'I am sorry', and perhaps draws breath. In addressing Angelo, Escalus is in a sense speaking to his equal, his mirror image (l. 463). He is not sorry that Angelo is to die, only that Angelo slipped (l. 465). Escalus is offended by Angelo's failure, because Angelo gave in to his desires and because he behaved so poorly afterwards. Escalus talks to him like a schoolmaster expelling a once-favoured pupil.

Angelo replies with a genuine sense of self-defeat – but to whom is his last line spoken? Escalus on the face of it, but perhaps it is also addressed to Marianna, or the Duke or Isabella. There are many possibilities here for the actors to explore. Who does Angelo entreat?

471–9   Having withheld a pardon from Angelo, the Duke now grants Barnadine an extraordinary act of mercy. Barnadine's entrance follows Angelo's entreaty: Claudio's face is hidden but the audience will recognize him and maybe Isabella starts to wonder too. Here, as elsewhere in the scene, the Duke makes little reference to his alter ego and instead appears to refer to himself as a friar in the third person. Barnadine, an anarchic presence on the stage, has no lines but still has the potential to steal the scene with either a disinterested or over-enthusiastic response to his pardon – either way, it seems unlikely that he stays onstage long or takes much advice from the other Friar to whose care the Duke leaves him.

Here the Duke is able to show the magnanimity and generosity that he withheld from Angelo. This makes a point: the Duke can dispense mercy if he is minded to do so. By releasing Barnadine, the Duke also further undermines Angelo's already discredited reputation: Barnadine is essentially being released in place of Claudio. But the whole speech is a sleight-of-hand trick, a distraction. The real question is: 'what muffled fellow's that' (l. 479)?

480–6   Claudio's unmuffling is a stunning reveal. The script begs for improvised dialogue here, mutterings of some kind, because no one says explicitly 'it really is Claudio'. Isabella and Claudio do not have any lines and no actions are noted, so the actors have immense freedom to explore the reunion of the two siblings. As both have been kept in the dark, surprise, love and shock are obvious, but there may also be more complex emotions at work – after all, they did not part on the best of terms.

The Duke's next line (l. 483) sounds like an acknowledgement of what is plain and obvious. Isabella does not ask for explanations – a long, silent stare may suit the character rather than a joyful embrace. Another option is for the Duke to take Claudio's hand and Isabella's hand. When he says 'give me your hand' (l. 485) he literally takes it, but he also means that he wants to marry her. Taking her hand there and then is a sort of contract, a 'thank-you' for reuniting her with Claudio.

Although he does not say so explicitly, the Duke is taking all the credit. But Isabella does not say she will marry him – in fact, she does not say anything at all. Does she even take the Duke's hand? Could she reject both the Duke and Claudio in this moment, the two who have manipulated her even more than Angelo, whose intentions were at least transparent? Isabella's silence here and for the rest of the scene can be played in so many different ways. The Duke does not know what to make of Isabella's silence. He must surely have been expecting more from this grand show, which now seems to be turning into an anticlimax.

487–91 The Duke now makes a wry comment about Angelo (l. 487), who has recovered from his penitent mood and is looking upon the scene with new hope. His 'quickening' eye snatches mercy before it is given. His earlier pleas for death were perhaps more shallow than they seemed. In the end, all the Duke does is rebuke Angelo and tell him that he must be a good husband.

492–505 Now the Duke turns on Lucio with anger that is either teasing or genuine (or both). If before Lucio was something of a comic foil, someone to play off against as the other characters learnt their lessons, someone against whom the Duke could maintain his pretence, then maybe now Lucio is once again picked on as a way out of a difficult spot. After all, we might expect the scene to continue with plots explained, siblings reunited, marriages laid out and celebrated. The turn to Lucio is symptomatic of the Duke's failure to produce a clean resolution.

506–16 Lucio's response parodies Angelo's. He admits 'the trick', and begs for mercy in a disarmingly matter-of-fact (but, in truth, hopeful) way. The Duke draws the Provost (again) into a deception. He enjoys threatening Lucio with whipping, hanging and, worst of all, marriage. After all that has happened, the play ends with an old joke about the miseries of marriage, as Lucio protests with more passion and worry than he did when he was simply facing execution. Lucio tries to curry favour by reminding the Duke that he made him and that he himself is a gentleman, not a Pompey-like clown. The Duke happily rescinds Lucio's punishments (did he ever really mean them?) but orders Lucio to be taken to prison to be married (and maybe he is back onstage with his wife by the end of the final speech).

As Lucio is led away, he makes a parting shot against marriage – he would rather be pressed to death (itself a suggestively sexual image) than marry. In performance, this is a sprightly and funny scene, a reminder that the play is a *comedy*. But Lucio's predicament, his misogyny and his pun on sex and death displace the real story. The Duke 'learns' mercy just as Isabella and Marianna did before him, but perhaps not with the same levity. The Duke enjoys himself when shouting to the poor Lucio, being led offstage, that he 'deserves it' (l. 516).

517–26 The Duke has the epilogue. His lines are straightforward: speaking to each character in turn, the Duke concludes their story and reminds them of their offence and punishment. Each character is addressed directly, the Duke presiding over the stage, his authority fully established, all loose ends tied up.

So much is clear – what is not so apparent is how each of the characters responds to the speech. Who did Claudio wrong, the woman he was to marry anyway? Why is marriage a punishment? Why did Marianna have to go through the emotional crisis of having to plead for her husband's life? – and so on.

526–end of scene   At l. 526, the Duke repeats his offer of marriage to Isabella but with typical caution. Yes, he has been manipulative. True, he may be no better than Angelo in exacting a sexual price for Claudio's life which, even though it may be more respectable than unmarried sex, is nevertheless quite different to the 'destined livery' of the sisterhood that Isabella imagined for herself at the start of the play. And it may be that Isabella has no real choice in the matter – how can anyone say no to a Prince? Yet the Duke is tentative and apparently sincere. The question of choice is never addressed, but he does not explicitly force Isabella into marriage and the play leaves open what happens next.

Isabella may react violently, with disinterest – there is plenty of justification in the text for an Isabella either finally repulsed or robot-ically subjected, her will crushed. Such interpretations will suit certain performance styles, but they do not suggest a rounded char-acter who has all along measured her honour against a fairly rigid value system, whose relationship with Angelo, twisted as it was, seemed to have some level of mutual desire. The woman who has nearly been a nun, nearly a whore, rejected by her brother as a sister, is now nearly a wife. And the Duke's offer is different to Angelo's – he offers her everything he has. Whether Isabella wants it is another matter.

One way to solve this problem is to leave the ending as ambigu-ous as Shakespeare does and let the audience judge what passes between Isabella and the Duke as these lines are said. The last couplet is probably addressed to one of the servants onstage – the entrance to the city continues, the place of justice mentioned, more revelations are promised, but there the play ends.

3 The Play's Intellectual and Cultural Contexts

Shakespeare's sources

Measure for Measure is based on George Whetstone's *Promos and Cassandra*, written first as a play and then as a novel (1578). Shakespeare would have also known Whetstone's main source, G. B. Giraldi Cinthio's *Hecatommithi* (1565). In the extract below, Whetstone summarizes his story in clear, sometimes colourful, language. Shakespeare made some changes, most notably introducing the Marianna subplot so that Isabella makes it to the end of the play with her chastity intact. He reduced the role of the accused brother Andrugio/Claudio and instead created a larger role for the King/Duke, who in Whetstone appears only at the end of the play. In the second extract, Cassandra visits Andrugio in prison to tell him about Promos's proposal. Shakespeare rewrites the scene in Act III, scene i. However, in his version the brother does not succeed in persuading his sister to save his life and, crucially, he introduces the Duke secretly watching the scene.

Instead of sensationalizing immorality as Whetstone does, Shakespeare turned to the Sermon on the Mount as a source for much of the play's political theory. The play's title directly alludes to it and many speeches echo its language, notably Angelo's when he justifies Claudio's imprisonment and the Duke's sermons to Juliet and, later, Claudio.

1 *From George Whetstone*, The History of Promos and Cassandra (1578)

The argument of the whole history

In the City of Julio (sometimes under the dominion of Corvinus King of Hungary and Bohemia) there was a law, that what man so ever committed Adultery, should lose his head, & the woman offender, should wear some disguised apparel, during her life, to make her infamously noted. This severe law, by the favour of some merciful magistrate, became little regarded, until the time of Lord Promos' authority: who convicting, a young gentleman named Andrugio of incontinency, condemned, both him, and his minion to the execution of this statute, Andrguio had a very virtuous, and beautiful gentlewoman to his sister, named Cassandra. Cassandra, to enlarge her brother's life, submitted an humble petition to the Lord Promos: Promos, regarding her good behaviours, and fantasising her great beauty, was much delighted with the sweet order of her talk: and doing good, that evil might come thereof: for a time, he reprieved her brother: but wicked man, turning his liking into unlawful lust, he let down the spoil of her honour, ransom for her brother's life: Chaste Cassandra, abhorring both him and his suit, by no persuasion would yield to this ransom. But in fine, won with the importunity of her brother (pleading for life) upon these conditions, she agreed to Promo. First that he should pardon her brother, and after marry her. Promos as fearless in promise, as careless in performance, with solemn vow, signed her conditions: but worse than any infidel, his will satisfied, he performed neither the one nor the other: for to keep his authority, unspotted with favour, and to prevent Cassandra's clamours, he commanded the Gaoler secretly, to present Cassandra with her brother's head. The Gaoler, with the outcries of Andrugio (abhorring Promos' lewdness), by the providence of God, provided thus for his safety. He presented Cassandra with a Felon's head newly executed, who (being mangled, knew it not from her brother's, by the Gaoler, who was set at liberty) was so aggrieved at this treachery, that at the point to kill herself, she spared that stroke, to be avenged of Promos. And devising a way, she concluded, to make her fortunes known unto the King. She (executing this resolution) was so highly favoured of the King, that forthwith he hasted to do justice on

Promos: whose judgment was, to marry Cassandra, to repair her crazed honour: which done, for his heinous offence he should lose his head. This marriage solemnified, Cassandra tied in the greatest bonds of affection to her husband, became an earnest suitor for his life: the King (tendering the general benefit of the common weale, before her special case, although he favoured her much) would not grant her suit. Andrugio (disguised among the company) sorrowing the grief of his sister, bewrayde his safety, and craved pardon. The King, to renown the virtues of Cassandra, pardoned both him and Promos.

2 *From George Whetstone,* The History of Promos and Cassandra *(1578)*

Act III, scene iv

Andrugio out of prison. Cassandra on the stage.

ANDRUGIO My Cassandra what news, good sister show.

CASSANDRA All things conclude thy death, Andrugio:
Prepare thy self, to hope it were in vain.

ANDRUGIO My death! Alas, what raised this new disdain?

CASSANDRA Not justice, zeal in wicked Promos sure.

ANDRUGIO Sweet, show the cause I must his doom endure.

CASSANDRA If thou dost live, I must my honour lose –
Thy ransom is, to Promos' fleshly will
That I do yield: then which I rather choose
With torments sharp myself he first should kill.
Thus am I bent: thou seest thy death at hand:
O, would my life would satisfy his ire,
Cassandra then would cancel soon thy band.

ANDRUGIO And may it be a judge of his account
Can spot his mind with lawless love or lust?
But more, may he doom any fault with death,
When in such fault he finds himself unjust?
Sister, that wise men love, we often see,
And where love rules, against thorns doth reason spurn:

But who so loves, if he rejected be,
His passing love to peevish hate will turn.
Dear sister then note how my fortune stands
That Promos' love, the like is oft in use,
And since he crows this kindness at your hands,
Think this, if you his pleasure do refuse,
I, in his rage (poor wretch) shall sing *Peccavi* [a confession of sin].
Here are two evils, the best hard to digest;
But whereas things are driven unto necessity,
There are we bid, of both evils, choose the least.

CASSANDRA And of the evils, the least, I hold, is death,
To shun whose dart we can no means devise;
Yet honour lives when death hath done his worst:
Thus fame then life is of far more emprise.

ANDRUGIO Nay, Cassandra, if thou thyself submit,
To save my life, to Promos' fleshly will,
Justice will say thou dost no crime commit,
For in forced faults is no intent of ill.

CASSANDRA How so th'intent is construed in offence,
The proverb says that ten good turns lie dead,
And one ill deed ten times beyond pretence
By envious tongues, report abroad doth spread.
Andrugio, so my fame shall valued be;
Despite will blaze my crime, but not the cause;
And thus, although I fain would set thee free,
Poor wretch, I fear the grip of slander's paws.

ANDRUGIO Nay, sweet sister, more slander would infame [make
    infamous]
Your spotless life to reave [steal] your brother's breath,
When you have power to enlarge the same;
Once in your hands doth lie my life and death.
Why that I am the self same flesh you are;
Think, I once gone, our house will go to wrack:
Knave, forced faults, for slander need not care:
Look you for blame, if I quail through your lack.
Consider well my extremity;
If other wise this doom I could revoke
I would not spare for any jeopardy

To free thee, wench, from this same heavy yoke.
But oh, I see else no way saves my life,
And yet his hope may further thy consent;
He said, he may percase [perhaps] make thee his wife,
And 'tis likely he cannot be content
With one night's joy: if love he after seeks,
And I discharg'd, if thou aloof then be,
Before he lose thy self that so he seeks,
No drought but he to marriage will agree.

CASSANDRA And shall I stick to stoop to Promos' will,
Since my brother enjoyeth life thereby?
No, although it doth my credit kill,
Ere that she should, my self would choose to die.
My Andrugio, take comfort in distress,
Cassandra is won thy ransom great to pay;
Such care she hath thy thraldom to release
As she answers her honour for to slay.
Farewell, I must my virgin's weeds forsake,
And live a page to Promos' lewd repair.

Exit

3 *From* The Holy Gospel of Jesus Christ, According to Luke 6: 28–38 *(Geneva Bible)*

Bless them that curse you, and pray for them which hurt you.

And unto him that smiteth thee on the *one* cheek, offer also the other; and him that taketh away thy cloak, forbid not *to take thy* coat also.

Give to every man that asketh of thee, and of him that taketh away the *things that be* thine, ask them not again.

And as ye would that men should do to you, so do ye to them likewise.

For if ye love them which love you, what thank shall ye have? For even the sinners love those that love them.

And if ye do good for them which do good for you, what thank shall ye have? For even the sinners do the same.

And if ye lend to them of whom ye hope to receive, what thank shall ye have? For even the sinners lend to sinners, to receive the like.

Wherefore love ye your enemies, and do good, and lend, looking for nothing again, and your reward shall be great, and ye
shall be the children of the most High; for he is kind unto the
unkind, and to the evil.

Be ye therefore merciful, as your Father also is merciful.

Judge not, and ye shall not be judged; condemn not, and ye
shall not be condemned; forgive, and ye shall be forgiven.

Give, and it shall be given unto you; a good measure, pressed
down, shaken together and running over shall men give into your
bosom; for with what measure ye mete, with the same shall men
mete to you again.

Jacobean politics and James I

In his speech to Parliament in 1603, James I introduced his reign by
describing the difference between a tyrant, who is 'proud and ambitious', and a 'righteous and just' King. James' political theory was
already familiar to many following the publication in England of
Basilikon Doron, a political tract originally written as a guide to being
a good king by James for his eldest son, Prince Henry. James I's formal
entrance to London in February 1604 was a major ceremonial occa-
sion and it was recorded by Gilbert Dugdale in his pamphlet, *The Time
Triumphant*. In this extract, Dugdale describes what happened when
James tried to enter the Exchange incognito. The disguised monarch
theme was used by more than one playwright that year, Shakespeare
included.

1 From James I, Speech to Parliament (1603)

I do acknowledge that the special and greatest point of difference
that is betwixt a rightful King and an usurping Tyrant, is in this:
That whereas the proud and ambitious Tyrant doth think his
Kingdom and People are only ordained for satisfaction of his
desires and unreasonable Appetites, *The righteous and just King
doth by the contrary acknowledge himself to be ordained for the
procuring of the Wealth and Prosperity of his People; and that his
great and principal worldly felicity must consist in their
Prosperity:* If you be rich, I cannot be poor; if you be happy, I

cannot but be fortunate; and I protest your welfare shall ever be my greatest care and contentment. And that I am a servant, it is most true, that as I am Head and Governor of all the People in my Dominion who are my natural Subjects, considering them in distinct ranks, so if we will take in the People as one Body, *then as the Head is ordained for the Body, and not the Body for the Head, so must a Righteous King know himself to be Ordained for his People, and not his People for him.*

2 *From James I*, Basilikon Doron (1603)

For the part of making, and executing of Laws, consider first the true difference betwixt a lawful good King and an usurping Tyrant, and ye shall the more easily understand your Duty herein: for *contraria juxta se posita magis elucescunt* [contraries are more visible when placed next to each other]. The one acknowledgeth himself ordained for his people, having received from God a burden of Government whereof he must be countable: the other thinketh his people ordained for him, a prey to his passions and inordinate appetites, as the fruits of his magnanimity. And therefore, as their ends are directly contrary, so are their whole actions, as means whereby they press to attain to their ends. A good King, thinking his highest honour to consist in the due discharge of his calling, employeth all his study and pains to procure and maintain, by the making and execution of good laws, the welfare and peace of his people; and as their natural father and kindly master, thinketh his greatest contentment, standeth in their prosperity, and his greatest surety in having their hearts, subjecting his own private affections and appetites to the weal and standing of his subjects, ever thinking the common Interest his chiefest particular. Whereby the contrary, an usurping Tyrant, thinking his greatest honour and felicity to consist in attaining, *per fas, vel nefas* [lawfully or unlawfully] to his ambitious pretences, thinketh never himself sure, but by the dissention and factions among his People; and counterfeiting the Saint while he once creep in credit, will then (by inverting all good Laws to serve only his unruly private affections) frame the Common-Weal ever to advance his particular: building his surety upon his people's misery: and in the end (as a step-father and an

uncouth hireling) make up his own hand upon the ruins of the
republic; and according to their actions to receive their reward.
For a good King (after a happy and famous reign) dieth in
peace, lamented by his subjects, admired by his neighbours,
and leaving a reverent renown behind him on Earth, obtaineth
the crown of eternal felicity in Heaven. And although some of
them (which falleth out very rarely) may be cut off by the treason of some unnatural Subjects, yet liveth their fame after
them, and some notable plague faileth never to overtake the
committers in this life, besides their infamy to all posterities
hereafter. Whereby the contrary, a Tyrant's miserable and infamous life armeth in the end his own subjects to become his
burreaux: and although that rebellion be ever unlawful on their
part, yet is the world so wearied of him, that his fall is little
meaned [lamented] by the rest of his subjects, and but smiled
at by his Neighbours. And besides the infamous memory he
leaveth behind him here, and the endless pain he sustaineth
hereafter, it oft falleth out, that the committers not only escape
unpunished, but further, the fact will remain as allowed by the
law in divers ages thereafter. It is easy then for you (my Son) to
make a choice of one of these two sorts of rulers, by following
the way of virtue to establish your standing; yea, in case ye fell
in the high way, yet shall it be with the honourable report, and
just regrate of all honest men.

3 *From Gilbert Dugdale, The Time Triumphant (1604)*

He [King James] came to the Exchange, . . . and thinking to pass
unknown, the wily Multitude perceiving something, began with
such hurly burly, to run up and down with such unreverent rash-
ness, as the people of the Exchange were glad to shut the stair
doors to keep them out . . . when his Highness had beheld the
Merchants from a Window all below in the walks not thinking of
his coming, whose presence else would have been more, . . . he
greatly commended them . . . but with all discommended the
rudeness of the Multitude, who regardless of time place or
person will be so troublesome.
[. . .]
And countrymen let me tell you this, if you heard what I heard as
concerning that you would stake your feet to the Earth at such a

time, ere you would run so regardless up and down, say it is his Highness pleasure to be private, as you may note by the order of his coming, will you then be public and proclaim that which love and duty cries silence to? This shows his love to you, but your open ignorance to him, you will say perchance it is your love, will you in love press upon your Sovereign thereby to offend him, your Sovereign perchance mistake your love, and punish it as an offence, but hear me when hereafter comes by you, does as they do in Scotland stand still, see all, and use silence . . . but I fear my counsel is but water turned into the Thames it helps not.

Moral tracts

Unlike *Promos and Cassandra*, *Measure for Measure* is not a moralizing play, but it does deal directly with some central moral preoccupations of the period. Christopher Sutton's *Disce Mori* is a typical example of many moral guidebooks to dying. This extract provides specific advice for those like Claudio and Barnadine who 'seem unwilling to depart the world'. Thomas Wright's *The Passions of the Mind* is represented by a brief extract in which Wright warns his readers that passions can supplant reason and blind judgement, a condition clearly suffered by Angelo. In his *Anatomy of the Abuses in England*, the prominent polemicist and anti-theatricalist Philip Stubbes gives voice to the common complaint that magistrates do not sufficiently enforce existing laws (the book is written as a dialogue, not a play). *An Homily of the State of Matrimony* is a standard Elizabethan tract on the importance of marriage.

1 *From Christopher Sutton*, Disce Mori – Learn to Die (1600)

How they may be advertised, who seem unwilling to depart the world

If in this life only (saith the apostle) we have hope in Christ, then are we of all men most miserable: to show in effect, that we have not in this life the accomplishment of our hope. Not here therefore we should expect it elsewhere: this is not our Paradise, but a barren desert: we may not look for our heaven here, our city is above which we all must inhabit, to argue back when we are to go most comfortably to take possession of the same, and the hope so long hoped for, should most strengthen us in the way, is far from that Christian belief whereof we make daily profession. Oft have we prayed, 'Thy kingdom come.' Now when God is leading us unto the same, our unwillingness to be gone cannot but argue great weakness of faith . . . What would we have done if God (saith Saint Jerome) had commanded us to die, without mentioning the resurrection, his will ought to have been our comfort: but now having this stay, why should we waver? Oftentime have we wished, that we were once freed from this world's captivity: now God is going about to free us indeed . . . There is no Mariner but after many sharp storms desireth the haven: and shall not we after so many tempests of this troublesome world, accept of our deliverance, when the time is come? We are given to love the world too much, and a great deal more, than we should, being only strangers in the same. Had we no farther expectation, but only to enjoy a state temporal, where we might set up our rest, as having attained our chiefest good, then might our departure from this world be very grievous in deed, because our being and happiness should end together. But looking as we do for a further condition, so permanent, so blessed, and Death being the passage of entry thereunto, there is no cause why man, if he bethink himself, should unwillingly set forward, when his time of departure is at hand. First remembering it is the ordinance of God, the course of all flesh, and, as Josiah calleth it, the way of all the world. What man is he (saith the prophet) that liveth and shall not see Death? It is not proper to anyone, which is common to all: kings, princes, strong, valiant, take part with them in this lot. There is no reason that any should look to be privileged in that wherein all without exception must . . . submit themselves. Secondarily, that it is a mean to bring us from a prison without ease; from a pilgrimage without rest, we all see evidently: and this made the Wise man praise the Dead above them which are yet alive, and prefer the day of death before the day of birth, surely for no other reason, than for that in the one we come into a vale of misery, in the other we depart from it . . .

2 From Thomas Wright, The Passions of the Mind (1604)

Passions blindeth judgement

Wise men confess, and ignorant men prove, that Passions blind their judgements and reason . . . As when the eyes are troubled, we cannot perceive exactly the objects of our sight; even so, when the heart is troubled, no man can come by the knowledge of truth . . . for in very deed, while the Passion is afloat, the execution and performance thereof, is conformable and very convenient unto our beastly sensual appetite, and therefore all beasts stinged by such passions, presently proceed unto execution, but men having united in the same sensitive soul, reason and discourse, are bound, both by the law of Nature, and commandment of God, divers times to repress and resist such unreasonable and beastly motions.

3 From Philip Stubbes, Anatomy of the Abuses in England (1583)

Spudeus. I pray you how might all these enormities and Abuses be reformed? For it is to small purpose to show the abuses, except you show withal how they might be reformed?

Philoponus. By putting in practise and executing those good laws wholesome sanctions, and Godly statutes, which have been heretofore, and daily are, set forth and established, as God be thanked, they are many. The want of the due execution whereof is *the* cause of all these mischiefs, which both rage and reign amongst us.

Spudeus. What is the cause why these laws are not executed, as they ought to be?

Philoponus. Truly, I cannot tell, except it be through the negligence and contempt of the inferior Magistrates. Or else, perhaps (which thing happeneth now and then), for money they are brought out, disfranchised and dispensed withal; for, as the saying is, *quid non pecunio potest*: what is it but money will bring to pass? And yet, notwithstanding, shall it be done invisibly in a clowd (under *benedicte* I speak it) the Prince being borne in hand that the same are daily executed. This fault is the corruption of those that are put in trust to see them executed as I have told you, and (notwithstanding) do not.

Spudeus. This is a great corruption & Abuse, and worthy of great punishment.

Philoponus. It is so truly; for if they be good laws tending to the glory of God, the public weal of the Country and correction of vices, it is great pity that money should buy them out. For what is that else, but to sell virtue for lucre, Godliness for dross, yea, men's souls for corruptible money? Therefore, those that sell them are not only Traitors to God, to their Prince and Country, but are also the Devil's Merchants and ferry the bodies and souls of Christians, as it were, in *Charon's* boat to the *Stigian* flood of Hell, burning with fire and brimstone for ever.

And those that buy them are Traitors to God, their Prince and Country also.

For if the laws were at first good (as, God be praised, all the laws in *Ailgna* [Stubbes' fictional country, a thinly-veiled England] be), why should they be suppressed for money? And if they were evil, why were they divulged, but had rather been buried in the womb of their Mother before they had ever seen the light.

And why were laws instituted, but to be executed? Else, it were as good to have no laws at all (the People living orderly) as to have good laws, and them not executed.

The Prince ordaining a law may lawfully repeal & annul the same again, upon special causes and considerations, but no inferior magistrate or subject what so ever, may stop the course of any law made by the Prince, without danger of damnation to his own soul, as the Word of God beareth witness.

And therefore, woe be to those men that will not execute the sentence of the law (being so Godly and so Christian as they be in *Ailgna*) upon Malefactors and Offenders!

Verily they are as guilty of their blood before GOD, as ever was *Judas* of the death of Christ Jesus.

4 *From* An Homily of the State of Matrimony *(1563; MacDonald 285)*

The word of almighty God doth testify and declare whence the original beginning of matrimony cometh and why it is ordained. It is instituted of God to the intent that man and woman should live lawfully in a perpetual friendly fellowship, to bring forth fruit, and to avoid fornication. By which means a good conscience might be preserved on both parties in bridling the corrupt inclinations of the flesh within the limits of honesty. For God hath strictly forbidden all whoredom and uncleanliness and hath from time to time taken grievous punishments of this inordinate lust, as all stories and ages have declared.
[. . .]

Wherefore, forasmuch as matrimony serveth as well to avoid sin and offence as to increase the kingdom of God, you, as all other which enter that stare, must acknowledge this benefit of God with pure and thankful minds, for that he hath so ruled yours hearts that you follow not the example of the wicked world, who set their delight in filthiness of sin, where both of you stand in the fear of God and abhor all filthiness . . . Which sort of men that liveth so desperately and filthily, what damnation tarrieth for them? Saint Paul describeth it to them, saying: 'Neither whoremongers, neither adulterers shall inherit the kingdom of God.' This horrible judgment of God you be escaped through his mercy, if so be that you live inseperately according to God's ordinance.

Prisons, brothels and constables

In *The Counter's Commonwealth*, William Fennor describes a debtor's prison not unlike the 'hole' in which Claudio and Barnadine are incarcerated. Fennor links the squalor of the dungeon with disease, and disease also characterizes Thomas Dekker's description of the suburbs and its brothels. Thomas Nashe castigates the city for its thieving prostitutes. All three passages evoke the seediness of London's underworld, yet each one probably exaggerates the degradation of the suburbs in order to make a moral point. They are

distant ancestors of today's red-top newspapers which use sensationalizing language to both condemn moral infidelity and sell newspapers. By contrast, Shakespeare is notably much more sympathetic
to the bawds, pimps and tapsters of Vienna's suburbs. The final docu-
ment here is a song which describes the difficulties of a constable's
life in the period.

1   *From William Fennor,* The Counter's Commonwealth *(1617;*
Judges 483–5)

He that would see the strange miracles of God, let him take some
long voyage to sea, and he that would see the miseries of man,
let him come into this place the Hole, that stinks many men to
death, and is to all that live in it as the dog-days are to the world,
a causer of diseases, except a few whom I have seen so stout and
tough (stink-proof, nay, plague-proof I think) that no infection
could pierce their hearts. Jerusalem when it was sacked had not
more calamities feeding upon her heart than this place, and I
think it was the true idea and shadow of this loathsome dungeon
where we live in, for as there was pinching famine in Jerusalem,
so in this place there are many men that for want of sustenance
utterly perish. In Jerusalem there was sickness, so in this place a
man shall not look about him but some poor soul or other lies
groaning and labouring under the burden of some dangerous
disease; the child weeping over his dying father, the mother over
her sick child; one friend over another, who can no sooner rise
from him, but he is ready to stumble over another in as miserable
a plight as him he but newly took his leave of. So that if a man
come thither he at first will think himself in some churchyard that
hath been fattened with some great plague, for they lie together
like so many graces. In Jerusalem the wars ruined millions of
souls; so in this place the continual war that hard-hearted credi-
tors makes against the lives of their poor debtors destroy many
wretched and most miserable creatures
[. . .]
This little Hole is a little city in a commonwealth; for, as in a city
there are all kinds of officers, trades and vocations, so there is in
this place, as we may make a pretty resemblance between them.
Instead of a Lord Mayor we have a Master Steward to oversee

and correct all such misdemeanours as shall arise. He is a very upright man in his dealings, though he stoop in his body. But the weight of the office he bears is the cause he bends, which is a great sign of humility.

2 *From Thomas Dekker,* Lantern and Candlelight, or The Bellman' Second Night's Walk *(1608; Judges 347)*

The infernal promoter being wearied with riding up and down the country, was glad when he had gotten the City over his head; but the city being not able to hold him within the freedom, because he was a foreigner, the gates were set wide open for him to pass through, and into the suburbs he went. And what saw he there? More ale-houses than there are taverns in all Spain and France! Are they so dry in the suburbs? Yes, pockily [with pox] dry. What saw he besides?

He saw the doors of notorious carted bawds like Hell-gates stand night and day wide open, with a pair of harlots in taffeta gowns, like two painted posts garnishing out those doors, being better to the house than a double sign. When the door of a poor artificer, of his child had died but with one token of death about him, was close rammed up and guarded, yet the plague that a whore-house lays upon a city is worse, yet is laughed at; if not laughed at, yet not looked into; or if look into, winked at.

3 *From Thomas Nashe,* Christ's Tears over Jerusalem *(1593; Steane 483)*

London, what are thy suburbs but licensed stews? Can it be so many brothel-houses of salary sensuality and six-penny whoredom (the next door to the magistrates) should be set up and maintained, if bribes did not bestir them? I accuse none, but certainly justice somewhere is corrupted. Whole hospitals of ten-times-a-day dishonested strumpets have we cloistered together. Night and day the entrance unto them is as free as to a tavern. Not one of them but hath a hundred retainers. Prentices and poor servants they encourage to rob their masters. Gentleman's purses and pockets they will dive into and pick, even whiles they are dallying with them.

4 · From James Gyffon, 'The Song of a Constable' (1626; Judges 488)

I a Constable have took mine oath,
    By which shall plain appear
The truth and nothing but the truth,
    Whos'ever my song will hear.
One Great Constable of England was,
    Another late should have been,
But little ones now 'tis found will serve,
    So they be but honest men.
A constable must be honest and just,
    Have knowledge and good report,
And able to strain with body and brain,
    Else he is not fitting for't.

Some parish puts a constable on,
    Alas! Without understanding,
Because they'd rule him when they have done,
    And have him at their commanding;
And if he commands the poor, they'll grutch [complain],
    And twit him with partial blindness;
Again, and if he commands the rich,
    They'll threaten him with unkindness.
To charge or compel 'em he's busy, they'll tell 'im;
    In paying of rates they'll brawl;
Falls he but unto do that he should do,
    I'll warrant you displease them all.

Whip he the rogues, they'll rail and they'll curse,
    Soldiers as rude 'cause they are,
Sent to the treasurer with their pass,
    And may not beg everywhere.
If warrants do come, as often they do,
    For money, then he it demands;
To everyone with 's rate he does go
    Wherein they are levied by lands.
They'll say then, he gathers up money of others
    To put to use for increase;
Else gather sit up to run away w'it:
    What terrible words be these!

4 Key Productions and Performances

Measure for Measure was hardly staged at all for centuries. The play puzzled critics and actors. Hazlitt, for example, complained that there was 'a want of passion' to engender real interest in the play's moral argument. Nineteenth-century audiences demanded spectacle but *Measure for Measure* lacked, or seemed to lack, opportunities to dazzle them. If the play was an extended moral debate, 'full of genius as it is of wisdom', as Hazlitt generously put it, there was *still* a problem, because the play's morality was confusing. Marianna gets to marry Angelo 'whom we hate', Isabella is too 'rigid' and the Duke too 'absorbed'. At some point in the twentieth century, attitudes to the play shifted as a series of performances, most notably Peter Brook's 1950 production for the RSC, showed that the play *could* be spectacular and that its moral complexity had something to say to modern audiences. Left to languish in the margins of the performance canon since the sixteenth century, *Measure for Measure* was recovered in the twentieth century as a very modern exploration of power and sexual politics: arguably, it is the most modern of all Shakespeare's plays and in the theatre it has been open to all manner of topical interpretations.

Making Shakespeare topical can be a risky business, but with *Measure for Measure*, the central questions about power, transgression and abuse have to resonate with the audience's own experiences. If they do not, then *Measure for Measure* is indeed a problem play, a character drama about unsympathetic characters. Fortunately, society and politics are rarely short of cultural materials to energize performance. To take one example, during the election campaign for the leadership of the Conservative Party in Britain in 2005 one of the candidates (David Cameron) was challenged over allegations that he took cocaine, because, as several newspaper editorials insisted, 'lawmakers cannot be lawbreakers'. The story took a further Lucio-esque twist when Cameron's closest political colleague was photographed with a prostitute called Madame Pain. Modern politics often returns to questions of how best to police desire, but the media is practised at exposing politicians' secret transgressions. In this environment, *Measure for Measure* has thrived. Sometimes productions make direct reference to topical events, but often they do not need to, for audiences are quick to identify with a playworld in which the demands of being a ruler and the pressures of being human frequently collide. When society was more deferential, and cynicism about politicians' sexual habits more restrained, *Measure for Measure* was rarely staged. Today, it is frequently performed: as attitudes to power have changed, *Measure for Measure* has reclaimed its status as a biting political satire that can address directly contemporary anxieties about the relationship between authority and its subjects. In recent years, the play has become more resonant than it ever was before and, in 2004, in the charged atmosphere following the Iraq war, there were no less than three productions in London, each by one of Britain's major theatre companies.

Social attitudes to gender and sexual politics have also made *Measure for Measure* feel like a very 'present' play. Before the 1960s, few in the theatre or in criticism worried much about what happens to Isabella at the play's conclusion. However, the sexual revolution of the 1960s made it virtually impossible to play Isabella without asking serious questions about what she wants and what she gets. John Barton's landmark 1970 production for the RSC established Isabella's reaction to the Duke's proposal as a crucial performance crux which most productions now engage with. In one production at the RSC in 1978, the actress Paola Dionisotti and her director Barry Kyle disagreed strongly over how Isabella should react to the Duke at the end of the play. Speaking to Carol Chillington Rutter, Dionisotti complained that her lines in the last scene were drastically cut because Kyle wanted a happy ending. Dionisotti could not see any happiness for Isabella: 'The energy of the language Isabella is using is a reflection of the enormous bank of strength she has in her. If a director deprives her of that language, he deprives her of her strength.' For Kyle, both the Duke and Isabella were 'happy' because they were able to leave behind the roles that had trapped them. He ended the play with the two alone onstage: 'the Duke bent down to retrieve the robe of justice Angelo had discarded. Then he left it there. She cast a long look at her fallen veil, then let it lie too.' Here was a subtle solution to the play's problematic silence, but by 1978 the time for such subtleties was past. Dionisotti was adamant: '. . . she *doesn't* give him his hand . . . Shakespeare is leaving an extremely big void here, a figure who goes completely silent and makes no commitment. She doesn't. He asks. But she doesn't.' (Rutter, pp. 39–40). Since 1978, happy endings have been rare. Modern audiences find it difficult to accept Isabella's silence as being anything other than a gesture of defiance to a political order which has done nothing but abuse her.

Modern productions also explore gender politics more explicitly. From Barton onwards, the dramatic confrontation between Angelo and Isabella in Act II, scene iv has been staged with increasingly graphic acts of sexual humiliation. Sometimes Angelo comes close to raping Isabella, only just holding back in time as he thinks of a more elegant way of getting what he wants. He has pushed Isabella, hit her; in some productions groped her, forced himself on top of her body or made her touch him. The degrading nature of these scenes naturally creates more sympathy for Isabella and pulls the play away from being a comedy. In the early twentieth century, directors and audiences would frequently articulate the 'problem' of *Measure for Measure* in terms of Isabella's dilemma: how could a (to them) modern audience accept that Isabella would sacrifice her brother's life rather than sleep with Angelo? But as the intensity of her scenes with Angelo has increased, this question has more or less vanished. Angelo is clearly a sexual predator, his abusive attitude towards Isabella physicalized. Angelo is the flipside of a society deeply wedded to sexual degradation. As theatrical mores have loosened, it has become common to add to Shakespeare's brief brothel scenes by filling the stage with prostitutes and staging simulated sex acts in the background to Act I, scene ii, and many add an extra scene to show the brothel being raided, its workers and their clients herded into police cells. Angelo's attempt to repress them is then read as an aspect of his own psychological repressions, which come out in full force in his fight with Isabella. Modern *Measure for Measures* frequently explore the perversity of sex in a Vienna which has thoroughly debased both politics and the body. Even Isabella's wild claim that she would rather be whipped than lose her honour has been interpreted as a sign that even Isabella has a kinky side (see Chapter 6).

The four productions I discuss here illustrate a rough history of *Measure for Measure* in modern times. I start with Peter Brook and John Barton because their productions are usually credited with shaping how the play is now performed. I will then conclude with two productions staged since the millennium that highlight different ways in which directors and actors have made topical the play's central preoccupation with power and desire at a particularly acute cultural moment, just after the Iraq war of 2003.

Roughness and dirt: Peter Brook

Peter Brook's 1950 *Measure for Measure* is regularly cited as the first major modern production of the play. Staged at the Shakespeare Memorial Theatre in Stratford (just a few years before the theatre was rebranded as the Royal Shakespeare Theatre), this production was instantly hailed as revolutionary. Laurence Olivier may have been exaggerating when he called it 'the most enlightening interpretation of any play' that he had seen (Weil, p. 28) but his enthusiasm was shared by reviewers and audiences. A tour in the then West Germany was so successful that a number of German productions followed. By 1970, when John Barton directed the play for the RSC, Brook's interpretation was the one to be measured against.

Brook's own account of the production remains one of the most incisive statements on the challenge of performing the play. In *The Empty Space*, he insists that *Measure for Measure* should be played, as it is written, in two registers in order to 'follow the movement' of the play from the Holy to the Rough (Brook, p. 100). Holy and Rough Theatre are Brook's own terms which he coined to characterize theatrical movements which resist 'Deadly Theatre', by which he means those productions (which we all have seen) which have no theatrical idea but lifelessly pay homage to the text without ever understanding it or wrestling contemporary meaning out of it. Briefly, Holy Theatre (which is not necessarily religious) attempts to go beyond the physical, whether into spiritual questions or into psychological states. By contrast, Rough Theatre belongs to folk culture; it is 'rough' because it is improvisatory and uncontainable, and can be played anywhere. It is also literally rough; it is very physical, sometimes violent, always bawdy. In terms of contemporary practitioners, Brook aligns Antonin Artaud with Holy Theatre, Bertolt Brecht with Rough Theatre. Brook's *Measure for Measure* is 'firmly rooted' in the 'disgusting, stinking world of Vienna' and, he continues, 'the darkness of this world is absolutely necessary to the meaning of the play: Isabella's plea for grace has far more meaning in this Dostoevskian setting than it would in lyrical comedy's never-never land'. In other words, the Holy and Rough do not simply coexist, one at court, the other in the stews and prison cells. Rather, the play depends on their interrelationship. Isabella's character only works because her story is contrasted with the grit and grime of the Prison and of Angelo's twisted authority. Brook utterly rejects any *Measure for Measure* which is 'prettily staged'; for him, to ignore the commons is to miss the point of the play completely. The play may be 'religious in thought' but it needs bawdy humour to make it 'alienating and humanizing'. Brook embraced the 'roughness and dirt', insisting that 'we must animate all this stretch of the play, not as fantasy, but as the roughest comedy . . . We need complete freedom, rich improvisation, no holding back, no false respect.' However, the demands of Holy Theatre also need to be respected and Brook cautioned against excess in staging those scenes written in verse which require 'less breadth, more intensity' (all quotes from Brook, p. 99).

Brook astonished reviewers by setting his *Measure for Measure* in a sleazy, grimy Vienna. Pompey, Lucio and Mistress Overdone owned the stage; it was their world which the Duke moved through in disguise, which infected Angelo and through which Isabella made her journey from nun to Duchess. Prior to this, productions consistently stressed the play's Christian themes and the commoners were often treated as little more than comic relief. Brook, then a young turk ripping up the rule books for Shakespearean performance, brought out the play's raw elements. The main parts were performed with dignity and intensity, but the ordinary characters had the play. They were not alone, either, as Brook populated the stage with 'prostitutes, beggars, cripples, and degenerates' (Venezky, p. 75) to create the feel of a bustling, decadent city long detached from those who sought to control it. Lucio, Pompey and Claudio could have been any of them; the Duke, diving in to the underworld, would have found many similar stories of clashes between Angelo's austerity and Vienna's liberality. So impressive was this spectacle that reviewers for years afterwards would complain when later productions had too few background characters. Robert Speaight thought the parade so vivid, its staging so energetic, that he expected them to start shouting 'Freiheit!' (freedom), perhaps recalling the recent liberation of German prisoners from the Second World War (Speaight, p. 246). Brook pushed the point to excess: there were parades filling the set of the prison (Weil, p. 29). George Rose played Pompey with 'bustling vigor' and 'leering amiability' (Venezky, p. 100). Not everyone warmed to Brook's innovations, but the reviewer for *The Times* was gracious enough to see that they were necessary, even if he found the brothel and prison clientele distasteful in Shakespeare: 'to like the play at all', the reviewer ruminated, 'we must be made uncommonly generous in our acceptance of ugly facts' (10 March 1950).

The only truly ugly fact was Angelo's hypocrisy. Angelo was played by John Gielgud in a performance that many at the time thought a definitive interpretation. Dressed in a bland olive-coloured robe, Angelo was a grave, unsmiling Deputy who was shocked when his own desires challenged his intellectual contempt for fornication. During the first scene with Isabella, Gielgud very subtly loosened Angelo's voice and made his gestures less surefooted. These were only the stirrings of a madness that eventually overtook the character; Gielgud showed it developing slowly as, layer by layer, Angelo's steady moral outlook was shaken by sexual desire. Angelo was not a born hypocrite, then, but a man in moral conflict unable to control, or even understand, what was happening to him. He was, as J. C. Trewin put it, a fanatic 'choked by the consciousness of his own virtue' (Trewin, p. 215). Gielgud played the final scene with a sombre dignity, kneeling to Marianna with what one reviewer called an 'eloquent silence' (Venezky, p. 75). Robert Speaight concurred; he thought that Gielgud's Angelo 'deserved that difficult forgiveness' (Speaight, p. 246).

It was the Holy Theatre rather than the Rough which dominated the final scene. In his reflections on the production, the scene that Brook focused on was in Act V, when Isabella pleaded for Angelo's life. This became the play's dramatic climax, displacing even the Duke's revelations in its impact. Brook daringly added a long pause before Isabella finally knelt with Marianna to beg for clemency. He instructed the actress, Barbara Jefford, to wait for as long as she thought the audience could bear, sometimes stretching the pause out to two minutes (an age in theatre time). Brook let the moral questions hang for a moment. Isabella was angry but, by deciding to forgive Angelo, she achieved a dignity unmatched by anyone else in the play. Brook called this silence a 'voodoo pole' around which 'all the invisible elements of the evening came together, a silence in which the abstract notion of mercy became concrete for that moment' (Brook, p. 100). Isabella's *other* silence, the one with which she ends the play, did not merit the same attention. On the contrary, the real drama lay in whether Isabella had the moral courage to ask for Angelo's life. The Duke's marriage proposal was, by contrast, a generic formality and Isabella's easy acceptance was wholly in keeping with Brook's conception of her as an early modern woman. The *Times* reviewer praised Brook for presenting Isabella as a woman 'consistent with the tradition of her age, her calling and her faith'. She was right to put her honour before her brother's life, right, too, to go along with the Duke's plans, and right, finally, to abandon a religious life for marriage (10 March 1950). Brook patterned Isabella's Holy Theatre character into a Job-like model of suffering. This was why it was so important to turn the play's climax on Isabella's plea for Angelo; it was her final challenge and, by begging for mercy, even when she thought Claudio dead, Isabella showed her mettle.

Brook's interest in the spirituality of the Holy Theatre extended to his interpretation of the Duke. Played by Harry Andrews in a performance that one reviewer dismissed as 'decorative', the Duke was a benevolent figure whose manipulation of the other characters was calculated to teach them moral lessons. Brook deliberately avoided questioning the Duke's motives for taking a disguise or letting Isabella think that Claudio was dead. Instead, Brook developed his religious theme by approaching the Duke almost as a Christlike figure who did not even lose his temper when goaded by Lucio, whom he defeated with a serene calm (Nicholls, p. 52). His soliloquy at the end of Act III, when he speaks in tetrameter and rhyming couplets about 'he who the sword of heaven will bear' (III.ii.222–44) was delivered as a 'moving' meditation on Angelo's failings and the problems of power (Venezky, p. 100). The whole production was 'Duke-centred', according to Weil, to the extent that some reviewers ignored Angelo and Isabella altogether (Weil, p. 29).

For audiences in 1950, *Measure for Measure* was still a relatively unfamiliar play. Productions before then were infrequent as the play was considered to be too dry and its central dilemmas too obscure for most modern audiences. Brook proved that this was wrong: the play could be gripping, its themes powerful, its characters complex and riveting. He showed how the prisoners, prostitutes and pimps could give spectacle to the play and, with his audacious pause, his 'voodoo pole', Brook opened up a new dimension of psychological uncertainty at the heart of the play's Holy Theatre-led drama.

Chaos in heaven: John Barton

John Barton's landmark 1970 production earned its place in theatre history for an ending that was, according to the director himself, widely misinterpreted by audiences and critics. Barton wanted to show Isabella lost in thought after the Duke's sudden marriage proposal. She had not even heard his first tentative reference to their marriage (a clever way to explain why the Duke talks of marriage again in his closing speech) and was stunned when the Duke forced his way between her and Claudio to solicit her 'willing ear' (V.i.28). With 'So bring us to our palace', the Duke and his crew left Isabella to ponder this extraordinary twist. Even this was a departure from a tradition in which the Duke saves the day through a series of spectacular *coups de théâtre* of which his marriage to the heroine (and why not, since he is the hero?) was the natural climax. Here was a much less forceful Duke, a bumbling and ineffectual figure. His proposal was garbled and nervous, and when it was met with silence, he played shyly with his glasses, looking 'sad and stoical' (Scott, p. 62), his hands trembling.

By closing the performance with Isabella alone onstage, Barton made the play hers, not the Duke's; and by ending her story with ambivalence, Barton created problematic questions about what has been achieved, and at what cost, at the play's conclusion. Critical responses jumped to the conclusion that the ending was dark, that Isabella was a crushed character. To some, this was heresy; but to others, Barton (however unwittingly) opened up a line on the play that made it suddenly very modern. With this 'shocking and brilliantly inspired new departure' (Gibbons, p. 160), what had been an odd little chamber drama about religious virtue and early modern political theory became, almost at a stroke, a play about a woman losing her struggle for self-determination. By playing out Isabella's unresolved doubt, Barton reminded audiences where she had come from, that she was about to become a nun, that she was going to withdraw from the world of men and words, and now, having successfully stood up for herself against an official who wanted to abuse her and a brother content for her to be abused, found herself being married to a man she hardly knew. Today, teachers will often begin with Isabella's silence as a problem – an unsolvable problem – which offers a way into the play for students who are more engaged by issues such as gender and sexual harassment than they are by religio-political debate. If one production can be said to mark the tipping point where Isabella's dilemma became the 'problem', then it was this one.

Barton was more interested in challenging the conventional representation of the Duke as a wise, just ruler. His Duke was played by Sebastian Shaw (an RSC stalwart who went on to play Darth Vader in *Star Wars*) as an ineffectual fool unable to master a situation for which he was partly to blame. He may have been 'a philosopher statesman' but he was also 'a pathetic, ineffective bumbler, lost and confused in the real world of men and affairs' (Nagarajan, p. 191). His first attempts at being a confessor to Juliet and Claudio were complete failures; Claudio ignored the sermon outright and ate his dinner instead. A short note in the souvenir programme by Barton's spouse, the academic Anne Barton, set up the Duke as a problematic figure by focusing on his many inadequacies. For example, she wrote, 'his attempt to stage-manage a human reality far too complex for such arbitrary ordering is inefficient. It also reveals his inability to understand the thoughts and feelings of other people.' In a famous quip, Anne Barton put her finger on an observation that now seems commonplace, but was then controversial: 'if the Duke is "an image of providence", there would seem to be chaos in Heaven' (quoted by Nicholls, p. 88). The Duke was not a skilful agent of justice but a dangerously incompetent ruler whose weaknesses were known well, as was evident when the court giggled mockingly at his decision to make Angelo his deputy. He was a ditherer, 'a pathetic figure' (Nicholls, p. 88). For Nicholls, the production's real achievement was that it exposed the extent to which it is the Duke himself whose indecision is the root of Vienna's problems (Nicholls, p. 63). Shaw played the Duke as a hesitant, ageing ruler who dressed in dark robes and a Holbein-style Tudor cap. The performance began with the Duke in his office, smoking his pipe, a clock chiming to register time passing, and surrounded by books which lay about his desk in disarray. After his departure, a fussy Angelo busied himself tidying the books up, blowing the dust off of them as he did so. They had clearly not been read or used for years; when Angelo assumed control in later scenes, the books were all put neatly away. The Duke was unable to focus on his responsibilities and disengaged from the city he ruled. As a friar, he continued to be an outsider and even in the final scene, the Duke seemed a distant figure. When Claudio (played by a raffish-looking Ben Kingsley) was revealed and Isabella held his arms as if to make sure he was real, the Duke stood, looking askance down Isabella's body, apparently jealous, and then pushed between them. Although at the time Barton insisted that he saw his production as 'Isabella's play', he cut the text and rearranged scenes in ways which largely served to give the production more opportunity to explore the Duke's problematic character (Nicholls 63).

Barton narrowed the play down to a chamber drama set in a large but empty room (designed by Timothy O'Brien) whose dark walls, made of inlaid wood 'like so many parquet floors' (as Wardle describes it) stacked upright, gave the production a gloomy, oppressive atmosphere. Peter Thomson noted that 'the perspective was sharply exaggerated, a distortion of the geometrical form it adumbrated', which he interpreted as 'a realisation almost of Angelo's mentality' (Thomson, p. 125). To create different scene locations, Barton and O'Brien used tables, small stools and chairs made out of thick, rough wood, adding to the production's sparse, 'poor-theatre' feel. Authority was signified by tall, high-backed chairs in which the Duke, Angelo and Escalus sat in the final scene. They looked rigid and uncomfortable, which was fitting given Barton's sceptical approach to the authority figures in the play. Bodies disappeared beneath costumes. All the 'court' characters wore dark robes which covered their bodies and tall, cylindrical hats which seemed to make their heads impossibly large. To register their political role, each member of the court had a coin-like design sewn into the middle of their robes, almost like a badge, robbing them of individuality. When Marianna entered in Act V to make her case to the Duke, she was completely wrapped in a shapeless, oversized hessian cloak with its hood obscuring her face. By contrast, the city characters were obviously at ease in their bodies; dressed in tight-fitting jackets and trousers, Lucio, Pompey and even Claudio were more obviously sexual characters. They and the 'city' set were sensual with other people, easily clasping each other in their arms and kissing, to the shock of the upright (and uptight) authorities who looked down on them as people whose sexual precocity needed to be reigned in.

Isabella belonged neither to the court nor to the city but was driven instead by what Irving Wardle called a profound 'sexual nausea'. Reacting against a tradition of mature, dowdy Isabellas, Barton cast a young actress, Estelle Kohler, whose youth brought a new dimension to the part. Her Isabella was immature but apparently sexually available, or so it seemed to the men who manipulated her, even to the Duke who was, in his disguise, her male counterpart, as both wore white religious habits that stood out against the set's dark backgrounds. Nicholls describes her as a 'moral show-off hiding her uncertainties about sexuality beneath a heroic protection of her virginity which bordered on the melodramatic'. This was a complex and unsympathetic portrayal of Isabella's hypocrisy. Far from being the most 'pure' character in a corrupted world, Isabella was a troubled figure whose 'masochistic comfort in rejection' prompted her to 'heights of rage' (Nicholls, p. 77). She was emotional, triumphant when she thought she had the better of Angelo, furious when it looked like he was going to get away with his abuses. She was petulant and stubborn; in one scene she was held back by guards but she still struggled to make her voice heard, railing at Angelo and the court. She was so overcome by Claudio's appearance in Act V that she fainted (and so missed the Duke's first proposal). This ambiguity fascinated Wardle, who noted the contrast between this emotional directness and her 'sheer coyness' which made 'the big scenes with Angelo and Claudio exceptionally rich in character development'. Her ambiguous, bewildered silence, alone onstage at the end of the play, led one reviewer to conclude that she was a 'frigid enigma' (*Birmingham Mail*, 2 April 1970). Penny Gay reacted differently; she saw Isabella as the only character in the play who ends it with dignity: 'as a living woman, in her plain white dress, with her long hair flowing freely down her back, she was a figure of personal integrity in a sordid world' (Gay, p. 129).

Angelo's hypocrisy was of a different kind. Where Isabella suppressed sexual desire with emotional directness, Angelo kept his emotions in strict check, only once breaking into tears when the Provost brought what he thought to be Claudio's head to him (an interpolated scene that the actors arrived at through improvisation). Played by Ian Richardson, Angelo was 'icy-cold' and 'slit-eyed' (Scott, p. 68). Reviewers noted that he was handsome, even 'beautiful' (Nicholls, p. 81), but drew attention to his emotional tautness: he was 'tight-lipped', his speech toneless, his habits 'fastidious' and 'clinical' (Thomson, p. 125), he kept wiping his hands as if pathologically afraid of being unclean (Nagarajan, p. 192). Wardle memorably described him as 'a marble embodiment of dehumanised logic' and for one reviewer he was a 'fallen angel', or perhaps a 'repressed chorister' (*Morning Star*, quoted in Nicholls, p. 81). What was repressed was, as Wardle put it, a 'savage child' whose violence came out in his second scene with Isabella when he 'advanced to her butting her with his groin'. He forced her on to his desk by grabbing her hair and ran his hand down her body, touching her breasts and stroking her crotch (this act was apparently Kohler's idea; see Gibbons, p. 68). As Nicholls puts it, Angelo's 'immature sexuality could only express itself in this brutal, unsophisticated way' (Nicholls, p. 81).

Measure for Measure was the last in a series of 'dark comedies' directed by John Barton following his earlier work on *All's Well that Ends Well* (1967) and *Troilus and Cressida* (1968). At the time, *Measure for Measure* was judged by most critics to be the weakest of the three. Irving Wardle thought it 'less than a knockout' and compared Barton's 'spare, intelligent, wary' production with Brook's 'riotous low-life spectacular' (*The Times*, 2 April 1970). Not everyone warmed to the 'Isabella rejects the Duke' ending and, with Brook's production still casting a large shadow (and Brook himself at the height of his powers, as the same season included his legendary *A Midsummer Night's Dream*), Barton's 'dark' *Measure for Measure* seemed overly gloomy and, with a small cast, an odd little chamber play. Yet Barton established a new theatrical afterlife for the play and, with hindsight, it was probably the most influential of his dark comedy trilogy. Barton's *Measure for Measure* was only the third production at Stratford since Brook's in 1950 (the other, in 1962, starred Judi Dench as Isabella). After 1970, the play became a staple and was revived several times in the following decade (the next production was in 1974).

The absurdity of authority: Sean Holmes

The RSC staged *Measure for Measure* in 2003. The director Sean Holmes initially struggled with the play, which he was not familiar with; like many, he found it difficult, its long two-hander scenes seemed too dry for modern theatre and 'the underworld of the play is quite opaque when you first read it'. I quote these comments because they strike me as typical of many actors and directors whose initial reaction to the play is that it is dull and difficult. Persevering with the play, Holmes began to realize what a dark and twisted work it really is and concluded that the only way he could bring it to the stage was to bring out its peculiarity. 'The point of the play is its oddity', he wrote, and to succeed, one has to 'to embrace the strangeness of it.' The strangest people of all were not the people in the underworld, but those who tried to regulate it. Holmes worked with the idea that each authority figure fails in some way, with the Duke being the biggest failure of them all. With the 'absurdity of authority' as his main theme, Holmes looked to absurdist tragicomedies as a model for thinking about his *Measure for Measure*.

Like Brook, Holmes approached *Measure for Measure* as an urban play. He compared the play's underworld characters to the 'prostitutes and drug addicts, police looking tired and armed and hassled' in the modern-day London's King's Cross area. Holmes set the play in a decadent, 1940s-style Vienna which he described as '*Third Man* meets *Taxi Driver*', referring to the post-war Vienna described by Graham Greene in his novel *The Third Man* and Martin Scorsese's 1970s film about alienation and obsessive violence in New York. In a revealing interview available on the RSC's website (www.rsc.org.uk), Holmes said that he wanted to show 'the real people of Vienna trying to live after a war' when 'there was prostitution for economic reasons'. City life was played against a large brick wall in the middle of the stage. An unscripted opening established the wall's function as a place for bartering sex and a means to conceal it, so that the Duke's first lines about governance were set against an atmosphere of easy subversion. Prostitutes came out from behind the wall with money to give to Mistress Overdone and, at one point, Pompey also entered the stage from behind it, greedily studying a handful of banknotes. The wall, monolithic and inescapable, seemed to represent a bankrupt authority. It worked as a dividing line between court and city; it was a place that concealed those seeking to evade authority but it was also used by the Duke to pry on Isabella and Claudio, whom he watched with just his eyes and forehead comically peeping over the top of the wall. For seasoned theatregoers, the wall might have recalled one of the most famous walls in recent British theatre: the wall which Lear obsesses over in Edward Bond's *Lear* and which stands in that play as a metaphor for oppression and the limits of power. Behind the wall, a cyclorama of sky and clouds suggested a world of freedom beyond the stage, but if so, it was a world which no one escaped to. For most scenes, and most characters, the wall defined them in some way. In one scene, it was the back wall of a prison, in another the wall of a train station, in another it was the edges of a moated grange.

The wall was the only substantial element of the set and the production's only nod to realism. Other scenes were created using the barest of props: a door and a desk represented Angelo's office; wired poles suspended from the flies mapped out a prison; Marianna's hideaway was just a chair, a tree, and a gramophone scratching out a 1940s ballad. This minimalism was affected by a Beckett-like sense of humour so that, for example, the monastery was evoked by a scarecrow, a wheelbarrow and two chairs, the prison's execution room by a guillotine and three sharp spotlights. On a stage as large as the Royal Shakespeare Theatre's, the lack of onstage clutter forced audiences to see the characters and their story in a stark relationship to the wall, which acted as a constant reminder of the absurdity of the events which happen around and behind it. To take a chair and call it a throne, or a few wires and call that a prison, in effect mocked Angelo and Claudio: both were trapped by their own inward blindness.

Holmes departed from recent stage tradition by putting his focus on the Duke rather than Isabella. He avoided an overly complex ending and even suggested a genuine attraction between them. At one point, Isabella seemed to forget herself, going to kiss the Duke (in his disguise) and then holding back, embarrassed to have shown such affection to a friar. In a later scene, the Duke held her hands paternally as he instructed her, but his hand lingered just a little too long. Suddenly realizing this, they stood away from each other, awkward and embarrassed. Such touches of innocence did not detract from what Holmes saw as the severe flaws in the Duke's character. He was not an ideal ruler, but nor was he a 'Duke of dark corners'. He was an absurd figure but he was not quite the bumbling fool of Barton's 1970 production. In fact, he was much younger than Shaw's Duke; he was a man with grand designs unaware of his own faults, who manipulated everything expecting to be celebrated as a great hero, only to crumble publicly as his people failed to give him the adulation he wanted. He was not a manipulator, in fact, events overwhelmed him.

He was unnerved when his bed-trick plot backfired; Barnadine ran naked round the stage refusing to be executed; and in the final scene, the Duke darted about the stage, frantically issuing orders. Meanwhile, as the truth emerged, other characters were very still. The Duke was the only person moving about, desperate now for some congratulation, some relief. This contrast between motion and stillness made him look lonely and isolated. Herded into couples, those in enforced marriages looked on confused and troubled, as if the Duke had suddenly gone mad. All stood awkward, refusing to be happy as the Duke clearly wanted them to be. Twice he held out his hands to Isabella, but she ignored him both times. Whatever there might have been between them had, it seemed, been betrayed. However, the effect of this was not so much to highlight Isabella's story as the Duke's, who was completely discredited by her refusal. The Duke was a tragicomic figure, isolated from those who he ruled, unable to relate to them and at his worst when trying to do so. Michael Billington thought him 'a fast-talking cynic with no fixed beliefs' (*Guardian*, 5 May 2003).

Holmes inverted the modern tradition of ending the play with Isabella or Isabella and the Duke alone; instead, Isabella marched the Duke into the wings and the lights went down on the rest of the cast, still onstage, looking shell-shocked. The Duke looked defeated; Isabella was off to have words with him. Isabella was finally showing some self-determination, something that in previous scenes she had been pushed into. In Emma Fielding's performance, Isabella was not naive, she certainly wasn't saintly, but she was deferential and loath to act. Lucio had to push her back towards Angelo when he first rebuffed her, a rejection which Isabella took all-too matter-of-factly. Marianna had to scream at Isabella to help her save Angelo's life. Isabella's hesitancy and self-doubt made her more like the Duke, who was similarly weak and unable to act decisively and with justice. They were naturally paired and obviously, though awkwardly, attracted to each other.

There was no such attraction between Angelo (played by Daniel Evans) and Isabella. Holmes avoided the erotic potential of their scenes to focus instead on Angelo as a cold hypocrite, almost inhuman, who at one point sniffed Isabella's neck like a vampire. At first,

Angelo was clearly disgusted by Isabella. She touched him lightly, hoping to persuade him to be more·lenient, but Angelo recoiled, apparently terrified of human contact. The memory of that touch evidently lingered, but the 'bad Angel' who bullied Isabella was not a sensualist, he was just violent. He pressed against her, brutishly offering himself, but Isabella's body was completely stiff and unresponsive. Angelo was a small, bald man with a thin moustache; he was a dour administrator who seemed to live behind his Gestapo-like rimless glasses, and was uncompromisingly vicious in his judgements. Paul Taylor made a shrewd comparison with 'the kind of functionary who, like Eichmann, might well have viewed the transportation of Jews to the death camps as primarily a logistical problem well suited to his organisational skills' (*Independent*, 6 May 2003). In other words, Evans' performance was a caricature of the ruthless, amoral bureaucrat. Such a narrow interpretation is possible, but runs the risk of making Angelo little more than a plot device. There was no good Angel in Angelo; he was always bad. Michael Billington was not convinced that Angelo had it in him to be much a threat to Isabella: 'although he twitches nervously at the sight of Isabella, you never sense the shock of a man of rigid principle overcome by sensual appetite'. So narrow was his world-view that he accepted his death sentence as sensible punishment, but was revolted by the Duke's pardon. At this point, the Duke seemed to be more of a hypocrite than his Deputy. Anxious to bring about a happy ending, the Duke tried to put Angelo and Marianna's arms together, but Angelo was a reluctant husband who found the charade excruciating.

Holmes was criticized for his 'moral negativism' (as Billington put it). As Movement Director Michael Ashcroft explains (in notes on the RSC website), 'one thing we know in this production of *Measure* is that it is cold. We also know that everybody is terrified of something. It is a very stark world.' The production had a Pinteresque menace, a brooding sense of violence which came out as black absurdist comedy in the Duke's bizarre attempt to butcher Barnadine. Ashcroft remembers that one of the keyword in rehearsals was 'vicious'. The production was made in the fraught political atmosphere of the invasion of Iraq; Holmes and his cast rehearsed as world leaders argued impotently over the rights and wrongs of military action, and the first performances ran as the invasion was launched. No wonder, then, that the production should focus in on a crisis of authority so bleakly. By setting the play in the 1940s, Holmes reminded audiences of Vienna's fascist past; in that context, the problem of tyranny was exposed as one of the play's central concerns. However, the Duke's filibustering tactics, his disengaged and ultimately disastrous attempt to bring order and humanity to Vienna, and his desperate effort to cheer up his miserable subjects, rendered the politics of intervention equally problematic. The Duke was an interventionist, his closing strategy pure 'shock-and-awe'. Although not conceived as an 'Iraq' production, Holmes' response to the play, one of the bleakest of those discussed here, showed him moving away from sexual politics towards the problems of order. *Measure for Measure* was on its way to becoming, of all things, a war play.

Sanctimonious pirates: Simon McBurney

In Simon McBurney's 2004 production (for the Royal National Theatre), the 'sanctimonious pirate that went to sea with the ten commandments' (I.ii.7–8) was George W. Bush, whose face flashed up on large television screens overshadowing the stage (so did Tony Blair's, so maybe there were two pirates). Like Holmes, McBurney wanted to explore contemporary cynicism about politics, especially in the wake of Iraq. But where Holmes had been subtle, McBurney was 'in-yer-face'. In the Viennese prisons, inmates wore orange jumpsuits just like the uniforms at Camp X-Ray in Guantanamo Bay and the outfits forced on to Western hostages beheaded by Islamic militants in Iraq (an association reinforced when the Provost hacked away at Ragazine's head behind a screen). Rarely had a production been so keyed to its moment. It caught the mood of audiences who were minded, it seemed, to embrace a play in which authority and manipulation are treated so ambivalently.

McBurney brought his own company, the Théâtre de Complicité, to the National to 'sex up' Shakespeare (to use a phrase much in vogue during the Iraq war when the British government was accused of 'sexing up' a 'dodgy dossier'). He did this in two ways. First, he brought a contemporary edge to the performance with a visually exciting set which was provocatively contemporary. The stage was populated with cameras, microphones and monitors. There were even television screens on the floor displaying hallucinogenic images that abstractly suggested different locations. Heavy pools of rain signified glum weather for the Duke's departure from Vienna, then luminous flashing lights changed the setting to that of a disco. For the next scene, the floor screens combined to show a huge painting of the Virgin Mary to signify the nunnery. Streaking lights and road markings suggested a night-time helicopter flight over the city; the Duke stood on a podium above this spectacle with a telephone, speaking to Friar Peter. Sometimes the floor screens were blank and only spotlights illuminated the main characters, imprisoning them with light.

The other way he sexed the production up was with sex. The production set out its stall in Act I, scene ii, which was set in a seedy disco. The Duke's attendants, who had been in the shadows in the first scene, became drunks dancing badly to loud modern house music. Some were watching porn videos on the television screens, rubbing their crotches distractedly. One man stood with his trousers down, being fellated by a prostitute on her knees, but there was nothing erotic about the act: he gyrated, then pulled away, the prostitute spat, wiped her face. He looked self-satisfied, she looked deadened, abused. From the beginning, sex was presented as abuse, an effective way to set up Angelo's behaviour towards Isabella.

Productions are sometimes crudely described as a 'Duke play' or an 'Isabella play' to indicate which story the performance privileges. This production staged Angelo's story. The Duke was too distant, too cruel a character to be the main centre of dramatic tension; Isabella was too abused to fill that role. Instead, McBurney centred the narrative focus on Angelo's psychological journey, which ended with a dramatic breakdown. Angelo was played by Paul Rhys as a damaged person haunted by his desires and barely able to keep himself together in the final scenes. His plans to bed Isabella were hastily made and not thought through, and afterwards, dealing with the consequences of embracing his desire, he behaved like a killer with a dirty secret which he was desperate to hide. Angelo was a charmless bureaucrat, young-looking, bookish, a kind of Al Gore figure keen to expose disorder and transgression. He was excessively ordered, even wiping a glass clean before drinking from it. In his first scenes, he talked through a microphone fixed to his desk. A close-up of his face was pictured on television screens behind him so that he looked like a lawyer at a congressional hearing. He gave every point excessive weight, every argument was related to wider issues, to big ideas. He showed no emotional interest in Claudio, only a politician's passion for justice as an abstract concept.

However, he was shaken by his first interview with Isabella. Isabella, in a strong performance by Naomi Frederick, was a head-strong woman, dressed in an anachronistically matched A-line skirt and wimple outfit. He sat in a businesslike leather swivel chair, his back to the audience but his face displayed in close-up on the screens so that the audience could study his reactions. To begin with, Angelo was unimpressed. Both characters looked drab. Isabella's hair was close-cropped and her hands were clasped as if in prayer. Angelo looked gaunt, his skin pale, his eyes and lips slightly reddened. He clutched at his microphone and turned away from Isabella, indiffer-ent to her suit and apparently disgusted by physical contact. Isabella retreated demurely but was pushed back onstage again by Lucio, who helped things along by pulling off her wimple and loosening the top buttons of her blouse. This got Angelo's attention. Kate Bassett describes Angelo watching her 'like a desperately repressed priest, pale as death and quivering' (*Independent*, 6 June 2004). After she left, Angelo tried to get up from his seat but shot back into it as if hit by electricity, his body twisting, his hands grabbing at his crotch with surprise and alarm, as if he had never had an erection before.

Angelo was horrified: sex disgusted him, but, he now discovered, he found disgust arousing. Isabella's 'ferocious absolutism' (as Paul Taylor put it), sexed up by Lucio, turned him on because her fervor was 'a distorted reflection of his own' (*Independent*, 31 May 2004). In their second interview, Angelo forced Isabella's hand into his flies so she could feel his erection: his discovery had to become hers. His seduction was sexual abuse, and like many abusers, Angelo was wrapped in guilt and denial. To Isabella, he appeared confident and menacing, but when she could not see him he was terrified, clearly out of his depth. To Marianna, who swapped her negligee for Isabella's wimple, he was a giant shadow looming over her on a stage shot with green light, his shadow filling the height of the back wall. However, behind the shadow Angelo was little more than a frightened boy. After the bed-trick, Angelo was jumpy and paranoid. He was a self-harmer as well, drawing a razor blade across his arm in an act which Taylor thought 'perversely orgasmic'. Angelo's demented self-punishment came to a head, literally, when he started carrying Ragazine's head around with him in a bucket full of blood, at one point thrusting his hand into the bucket and smearing blood across his shirt. Rather than take the shirt off, he concealed it with his suit jacket: this became a symbol of his guilt which the Duke dramatically uncovered. Angelo had curled up in his chair in a foetal position like a naughty child hiding from its parent. The Duke angrily swung it around and pulled Angelo by the scruff of his neck out of the chair, forcing his arms open so that his jacket fell lose to expose his blood-stained shirt: his guilty secret was out. Later, readying herself to plead for Angelo's life, Isabella stared at him for a moment that suggested an unexpected tenderness. Angelo and Isabella ended the play next to each other on the stage, never destined to be a couple, yet so clearly alike.

David Troughton's Duke was an inscrutable ruler; Charles Spencer called him 'boomingly sadistic' (*Daily Telegraph*, 28 May 2004). As an RSC veteran, Troughton seemed out of his element in a *Complicité* production which prioritized striking visual images over verse speaking. He turned this to his advantage; he was a brooding outsider in his first, rain-soaked scene, huddled moodily under an umbrella as he waited for his helicopter, garrulous and Lear-like. The Duke was an outsider, too, in his final scene, which he made a cruel trick by a ruler who seemed to have no wish to relate to any of his subjects, each of whom he treated with contempt. As the Friar, the Duke looked frightening, gaunt and pale, his face hidden under a black habit. Troughton used disguise as a starting point for his characterization. In his first scene, he used a cane to help him walk, but this limp was put on. As the Friar, the Duke walked confidently, his limp only returning when he became the Duke again. This was a

Duke who was constantly in disguise, always wearing masks. For his first scenes, the Duke avoided interacting directly with other people. He treated Escalus, who ran after him anxiously in the first scene, with world-weary indifference. Friar Peter spoke to him by telephone, the Duke's interview with Claudio was conducted via microphone, and the Duke eavesdropped on the siblings with television screens. He avoided intimacy and was unaffected by human bodies; he was not even agitated by Barnadine. There were some comic moments: the Duke revealed himself to the Provost by suddenly pulling down his hood, but it was the Provost who turned the exchange into slapstick with a dead faint. In the last scene, now playing the Duke again, he hobbled onto the set and sat on a chair, physically imposing and diffident, avoiding eye contact. The response to his first big reveal was electric; everyone onstage immediately threw themselves prostrate on the floor. However, as each story played itself out, the depth of this devotion was tested. Barnadine, a large, fat old man with a grey beard and unkempt hair, his prison clothes defiantly pulled down to his waist, stopped on his way out before the Duke and stared intensely at him for a beat, as if not sure whether to hit him or hug him. The threat of physical intimacy, violent or not, affected the Duke, who looked troubled and uncertain for the only time in the performance.

The Duke was not playing a game; his threat to kill Angelo, his contempt for Lucio, were both real and vicious. As Taylor points out, the Duke brought about 'a "happy" ending as much by intimidation as by effecting a change of heart in others'. Lucio was held down by a guard next to his bride; another guard held a pistol to Angelo's head about to lead him off to execution. For Isabella, who already looked petrified, the Duke offered his hand and then stepped back to reveal a small chamber at the rear of the stage in which was a brightly lit white bed. Isabella was at the front of the stage, kneeling, her head turned back, her mouth gaping, so enacting the silence that Shakespeare wrote for her (and Angelo doing the same). The Duke was in the middle left, stooping, his hand stretched out towards the bed. The Olivier is a big stage, according to theatrical legend designed by Olivier to destroy any actor who acted on it, so these spatial differences created a real impact: suddenly attention was thrown on the bed in the distance, the Duke isolated in the middle of the stage, the rest of the cast sharing the audience's view of these two lonely scenes, the Duke and his empty bed.

Conclusion

The four productions discussed in this chapter demonstrate how varied and provocative *Measure for Measure* can be in performance. Although Brook and Barton are rightly celebrated for their work, there were many productions around the world that explored similar themes. Since the 1970s, there has been an astonishing breadth of interpretations, some measured and conservative, others bold and experimental, and many which try to be adventurous without leaving behind their audiences. Holmes and McBurney have shown how appropriate *Measure for Measure* is as a black comedy which can reflect on troubling anxieties in modern society, but companies such as Cheek by Jowl and Shakespeare's Globe have staged recent productions which prove that a more actor-focused approach can still make of the play a riveting drama. One need not subject the play to McBurney's shock tactics to make it contemporary and accessible. Shortly before this, the National Theatre toured a very experimental production that adapted the play to suit the forum-theatre methods pioneered by the Brazilian director Augusto Boal, in which audiences were invited to debate the issues raised by the play during the performance and even make collective decisions about the progress of the story. *Measure for Measure*'s strength is that it presents crucial social dilemmas about power, gender, and so on in ways which are adaptable to present circumstances; yet it is also a powerful character drama and its many 'problems', from puzzling the Duke's motives to understanding Isabella's silence are, in performance, powerful cruxes through which theatre companies can work out their own interpretations.

5 *The Play on Screen*

Even though its themes are surprisingly contemporary, *Measure for Measure* has never been filmed (not in English at any rate – there was an Italian version made in the 1940s, but the print is believed lost). This is surely a missed opportunity, as the play is certainly a more promising prospect for the cinema than *Love's Labour's Lost*, *2 Henry IV* and *Titus Andronicus*, all of which have been made into films. In an age when American presidents are impeached for lying about sexual affairs, when the media trades on kiss-and-tell stories, there is plenty of cultural material about to make a stunning *Measure for Measure* film – but since Hollywood producers are also frequently accused of using their casting couches for sexual bargains, perhaps such a film would hit too close to home.

Television has been more adventurous. The two films which I discuss in this chapter were both made for the BBC, albeit under very different circumstances. The first I will discuss is Desmond Davis's contribution to the BBC–Time Life Shakespeare series. Made in 1979, Davis's film suffered from an overly conservative approach to Shakespeare which marred the early contributions to that series. Nevertheless, this film has some real strengths and it is generally regarded as one of the more successful adaptations which the BBC produced in the 1970s. It is also the most widely available film version of *Measure for Measure*; most university libraries hold copies and it can be bought on DVD.

Harder to find is David Thacker's 1994 television film made for BBC2 and only broadcast once. Some university archives carry off-air recordings and those in UK universities can borrow copies from the British Universities Film and Video Council (http://www.bufvc.ac.uk). The production is well worth the effort to find, as it is the most daring film there has been of the play, and the only one to see in it a dark satire of contemporary media politics. The film makes for a striking contrast with Davis's version for, where Davis took only a few risks and played the text as straight as he could, Thacker explored the relationship between media, sex and power. Davis brought Shakespeare to television and did what he could to make television accommodate a work originally written for a public theatre. Thacker brought television to Shakespeare and sacrificed key parts of the text to cut Shakespeare to a more modern cloth.

Resisting tradition: Desmond Davis

Desmond Davis appeared to reject (or perhaps, more simply, ignore) the advances in interpretation made by John Barton and others in the theatre earlier in the decade. As a result, the film was stagy and sometimes very static: it looked like a televised version of the kind of picture-book shows that characterized productions in Stratford-upon-Avon in the 1950s. Davis and his cast relied on a style of performing Shakespeare that was recognizable to them and to their audience as 'traditional' Shakespeare. This was intentional and it was a style in keeping with most BBC Shakespeare productions in the 1970s that favoured mock-theatricality over the naturalism in most television drama. For example, set backdrops were obviously painted backgrounds. Television drama is practically never so obvious about its artifice (why paint a background when you can film it?), but for this film a painting of the moon and stars signified it was night; another large painting of a red sky indicated it was morning. Given that *Measure for Measure* can easily be played as an entirely interior play (as Thacker did in his film), the use of these backdrops can only be explained as brazen deference to the perceived authenticity of traditional Shakespeare performance.

However, to be fair to Davis, he was doing no more than fulfilling the brief that had been given to him. The series was the product of an innovative partnership between the BBC and Time-Life; a stipulation in the contract between the two companies specified that there should be none of the experimentation associated with modern

theatre. Davis's *Measure for Measure* was commissioned and broadcast
under the tenure of the original producer, Cedric Messina, a man
whose Shakespearean sensibilities were no less traditional than those
of the corporations'. Messina made sure that directors steered clear of
modern dress, fast cuts and any experimentation, theatrical or televi-
sual. He also ensured that, as per the brief, the film was free of 'interpretation' which is, of course, a nonsensical proposition but reflects
the artistic presumptions which contextualize the production (see
Susan Willis's excellent book on the BBC Shakespeare series for more
about this agreement). What this meant in practice was that Davis
could not use the play to make allusion to contemporary issues.

Consequently, the period-setting was as far from the present as it
could be: not quite the sixteenth century, more like a pantomime
memory of it. All the men were bearded and wore hats, doublet and
hose. The clowns pranced about if they were dandies, spoke with
Lancashire accents if they were idiots and if they were 'common',
slouched their shoulders and screwed their faces up in childish
disgust. Lucio's face was pale, his cheeks polished with rouge;
Pompey's face was covered in grime, his hair dishevelled. All characters wore the same outfits for the whole production (even though the
play should take place over several days) and the actors performed to
each other as if they were on stage, the two cameras filming almost
as eavesdroppers.

Yet all this was a superficial gesture of deference towards 'pure'
Shakespeare. Davis, who had started his career working on British
realist films such as *A Taste of Honey* (1961) and *The Girl With Green Eyes*
(1963), was not an armchair traditionalist. Although he stayed firmly
within the BBC 'house style', Davis showed each of the main characters struggling with sexual incompetence. The Duke was not an 'ideal
ruler' sagely testing his subjects, nor was he a 'good father'. On the
contrary, as played by Kenneth Colley, he was an anxious ruler, a
small man often ignored by those around him, who wore an absurdly
large gold seal around his neck to signify his power and, in the final
act, indulged himself in public spectacle. In both his first and last
scenes, the Duke was surrounded by courtiers and sycophants
(Angelo had no courtiers around him, nor did he wear a seal of
office). With insincere modesty the Duke insists that he does not like

to 'stage me to their eyes' in the first scene, then in the last scene arrives on horseback like a returning hero to a cheering mob. Davis framed some camera shots to show up the Duke's indifference to those around him. For example, when the Duke (as the Friar) lectured Claudio in his cell, Davis kept his camera focused on Claudio, who was not listening to his confessor at all. The Duke pontificated in the background, bobbing absurdly behind Claudio's back like a hyperactive salesman. The more the Duke spoke, the more detached Claudio became, but the Duke didn't notice as he was too busy enjoying playing the role of a bossy, ghostly father. Camera shots framed a similarly ironic juxtaposition of the disguised Duke meeting Escalus (which Davis set in Mistress Overdone's brothel after it was raided). Colley played this scene as the moment when the Duke realized he could find out what his subordinates really thought about him. Again, the camera was held on Escalus even when the Duke was speaking. At first, the Duke hid his face with his cloak but as he grew more confident and more self-absorbed, he risked letting his face show and asked ever more pointed questions about himself. The camera closed on Escalus' careworn face, its interest in foregrounding him visually contrasting with the Duke's anxious self-obsession. By focusing the shot on Escalus rather than the Duke, Davis subtly called attention to the Duke's own failure to take any interest in the man – his questions were all about himself.

All of the men were weak and under-confident. Escalus was sagely detached, Lucio was a prancing dandy, Pompey a grimy lecher, Claudio a petulant (and then scared) adolescent. Angelo was the worst of them all, as if all the faults of the other men in charge in Verona were distilled in him. Tim Piggott-Smith played the prenzie as a smug young buck dressed in black like a pantomime villain. In his first scene, he was authoritarian, sweeping a new broom through the Duke's lazily decadent court. However, there were early hints that Angelo's hardline stance was hypocritical. His court may have been more spartan than the Duke's, but it was sumptuously decorated with sensuously patterned rugs liberally draped over tables and hung on walls. Most strikingly, on a pedestal at the main entrance, there was placed a large statue of a naked man coyly twisted so that his genitalia pointed at anyone coming through the doors. When

Isabella came to make her plea for Claudio's release, she had to contend with this extraordinary sight first. After his first interview with Isabella, Angelo started to look like a bohemian bachelor. He became unkempt, dishevelled; his shirt was carelessly buttoned to show his chest-hairs and the ladykilling gold medallion which he wore (the Duke wore a medallion to symbolize his civic power; Angelo's represented his sexual power).

Davis may not have been able (or maybe willing) to see in the play the kinds of sexual complexities that Barton and subsequent directors explored in the theatre, but, without ever really pressing the point, he presented the play's women as strong people with little self-doubt trying to survive in a society ruled inadequately and hypocritically. Marianna, played by Jacqueline Pearce, was a determined and sensual Pre-Raphaelite woman who, in the last scene, briefly dominated the play with a riddling story which baffled and horrified the men who listened to it. Kate Nelligan played Isabella as an inwardly tough young woman who naively believed that Angelo would help her, that Claudio would respect her, that the Friar would save her, yet ended up resisting each of them. In her first scene, already being pressured by a man (Lucio), Isabella was thoughtful but inscrutable, neither resisting Lucio but not giving anything away either. She was the same with Angelo, with whom she stood with her hands clasped.

Although Davis would never have got away with Barton's bold ending where Isabella rejected the Duke's offer, he and Nelligan found another way to end Isabella's story. Claudio and Barnadine were brought onstage, both manacled, their faces hidden by sacks. When Claudio's face was revealed, the Duke's final trick played out, Isabella joyfully hugged her brother: but both stopped and stared with surprise at the Duke when he made his proposal. Isabella was left in the background again, mulling over her situation. Nelligan made a virtue out of the Duke's second reference to marriage in his final speech to give Isabella time to make what was really a political rather than personal decision to be the Duke's wife. He held out his hand and she looked blankly for a moment as if she were weighing up the situation. By allowing Isabella this pause, by not instantly taking the Duke's offer, Davis and Nelligan gave Isabella some self-determination. Then her face transformed: where she had been stony, now she was sunny, where she had been demure, now she was charming. Her prior blankness and her sudden change of mood signalled that this was an act. She slipped into the role of the courtier queen and walked off stage with her new husband, following the other married couples: Claudio with Juliet and her baby, Angelo with Marianna. The BBC–Time Life partnership had the happy ending it wanted.

Duke of dark corners: David Thacker

In 1994, the BBC broadcast David Thacker's version of *Measure for Measure* as part of its 'Performance' strand, an occasional series of films based on plays written for the theatre. Unlike the BBC Shakespeare series, Performance did not impose any particular style or agenda on its directors so Thacker had a lot more freedom to develop his own vision for the play than Davis. Where Davis was constrained from departing from the text, Thacker was able to do what he liked with it. He cut key characters, reassigned lines to new characters and cut up scenes into smaller chunks so that the story could move more quickly between different parts of the story. By doing this, Thacker made the play feel more like a work written for television rather than the theatre. The film also looked very different to Davis's. It was set in a world which mixed elements of the past and the present: police officers wore contemporary uniforms, Angelo and his retinue wore tailored suits and looked vaguely Edwardian, Lucio looked like a 1950s spiv. Discordant, futuristic music opened the film.

Thacker was also a much more accomplished theatre director than Davis and was a former Artistic Director of the Young Vic, where he had directed a modern-dress *Measure for Measure* in 1987. For that production, Thacker signalled his approach to the play by inviting Richard Wilson, an academic who has written extensively on Shakespeare and Michel Foucault, to write an introduction for the show's souvenir programme which discussed the relationship between power and surveillance. As television is a modern surveillance technology, the same ideas lent themselves well to a television version of the play and the first shots of the film introduced television itself as a reference point. A moody opening shot of the Duke slumped on a sofa watching a huge bank of televisions established the surveillance theme. He sipped whisky disconsolately and was surrounded by books in a darkened room, his eyes red as if he had been up all night obsessively watching television. On the screens flashed a series of images of urban sex and violence: a prostitute walking the streets, an illegal fight, and so on, each image flicking to the next with no apparent logic.

Tom Wilkinson played the Duke as a world-weary melancholic obsessed with watching people and frustrated at his own impotency as a spectator. Barely making eye contact with Angelo and Escalus, the Duke slouched off for a fraught meeting with a friar, a scene played in close-up with the Duke anxiously wringing his hands and then clutching his forehead as if unable to confront life at all. A similar melancholia emerged when he counselled Claudio, who readily nodded in agreement at the Duke's despairing reflection on the pointlessness of life. A turning point was reached when the Duke retreated to the Provost's office to watch Isabella and Claudio on his CCTV monitor. Thacker again focused on the Duke's response as a watcher, particularly when Isabella revealed Angelo's proposition. This was clearly a shock, one which jolted the Duke out of his stupor and propelled him, for the first time, into action. What had been a dreary, masochistic descent into the hell he had witnessed on the television now became a mission to intervene and restore justice. But the Duke's final scene returned to the world of television; his office was transformed into a television studio, cameramen followed each speaker and those waiting to be admitted watched the live feed on monitors in an antechamber and in the Provost's office. The Duke began as a spectator, became an actor and finally revealed himself as the director of the whole show when he took off his friar's habit and banged his fist on the table to mark out the metre of his keynote speech with bitter anger, 'measure for measure' (V.i.404).

To begin with, Angelo was a 'breath of fresh air' who, unlike the Duke, had no qualms about exercising his authority. Where the Duke was lethargic and pacified by drink, television and too much thought, Angelo was straightforward, active and keen to do business. They were opposites, but perhaps also two sides of the same coin: the Duke representing an authority that only ever watches, Angelo one which never watches but only acts. This characterization was signalled early on. With the Duke gone, Angelo stepped round the gloomy office. He put away the Duke's whisky bottle which had rolled onto the floor and stared for a moment at the television screens still showing seedy films before turning them off with a remote control. Then he picked up one of the books from the floor, shaking his head as if not knowing where to start. Angelo was a second-in-command who finally had the power that he had so long seen frittered away by a master who was in a rut; he looked at the book and the screens with a mixture of contempt and triumph. He then walked over to the desk, thought again for a beat, then with a sudden spread of his arms, swung back large shutters barely visible in the gloom at the back of the office, letting sunlight in. This was a strong *coup de télévision* and a viewer who did not know the play might well expect great things from this Deputy. A scene later the books were tidied, the drink had vanished, the desk was empty apart from one large ledger, and the bank of televisions had been removed to reveal a stone fireplace. There was only one dissonant note: sitting at his desk, Angelo briefly contemplated a picture of himself and Marianna, this juxtaposed with a cut to Marianna staring out of a rain-smeared window. He dropped the photo into a drawer and shut it, as if Angelo's firm authoritarian personality concealed unfulfilled desires.

Thacker contrasted Angelo's assumption of authority and the Duke's despairing sabbatical with the lively world of the brothels. He edited the script to allow for more rapid cuts between scenes, so that Act I, scene i was split into several scenes intercut with Lucio and Pompey in Mistress Overdone's brothel. The brothel was as dark as the Duke's office but it was bigger. As Lucio argued with two prostitutes (with lines cleverly adapted from the two Gentlemen Lucio banters with in the play), Mistress Overdone sagely sat at a bar smoking from a long cigarette, nursing a baby and somehow retaining her dignity despite the chaos around her, even when one girl staggered from beneath the bar and threw up at her feet. In the background, her customers watched porn films with the same kind of detachment as

the Duke in the first shot. Having established these two worlds, with
Overdone and the Duke curiously similar figures both in charge but
letting hell break out around them, Thacker then showed the same
world as it was brought to heel under Angelo. Police raided a restau-
rant to arrest Claudio, brutally pushing his face into the table and
dragging him away from a romantic meal with Juliet. Later, police
broke into Overdone's nightclub en masse, grabbing half-naked men
and women and herding them out into the street. The police station,
to which these characters were now taken, was a drab, grey office,
humourless and sterile. The police gathered to watch as Claudio was
stripped in a side-office. The Provost snapped a rubber glove on to
his hands as Claudio, naked, bent over to be 'inspected'. Later, prostitutes made a play for the policemen and half-dressed, overweight
men dug through a pile of clothes. Isabella peered through a window
looking at the rabble before being gently led away by the Provost.

Isabella emerged as the only moral force in a world caught
between depressive liberality and oppressive surveillance. Thacker
introduced her early on, making her part of the panorama of establishing shots before she came into the story. She was in a nun's cell,
almost as bare and claustrophobic as the one Claudio was pushed
into in a parallel shot, and she was having her hair cut, long locks of
it stretching to the floor sliced off by another nun. Isabella was trying
to escape from the world. Her hair was roughly cropped and she
wore not a habit but a simple hessian dress tied at the middle. She
looked like Joan of Arc. With Angelo she pushed a little, then a little
more, trying to find the right words to say until, in desperation, she
seemed to tear the words from somewhere inside herself, twisting
her body almost as if possessed. All of the men in the office with her
were fascinated: Angelo was entranced.

It was at this point that Thacker's initial opposition of the Duke's
depressive impotency and Angelo's ruthless but effective efficiency
was turned on its head. The Duke may have watched his city's vices
in despair, but with Angelo the sexual desires that he tried to police
in the city emerged with violent force in his own attraction to
Isabella. The fire was now lit and flickering red light around the
room; two sofas placed facing each other with the fire between them
to create an atmosphere of relaxed intimacy: the office had become

Angelo's lair. This was where Angelo took Isabella when she came to ask him once more to let her 'bribe' him. Angelo sat on one of the sofas and listened carefully as Isabella made a fresh plea which this time was not a public accusation as before, but an intimate exchange. Kneeling on the floor by the fire, she touched his legs, stroked him, looked up at him wide-eyed, her face close to his, and she spoke to him like a daughter trying to manipulate her father. Angelo was ill-equipped to turn a date into a full sexual encounter. He struggled with his words, wanting to be direct but not knowing how to be so. For a moment, it was Angelo who was the sexual innocent, Isabella the manipulator. But this soon changed as Angelo clumsily pressed on and impatiently brought things to where he imagined they were always heading. The conversation reached an impasse when Angelo softly pointed out Isabella's false logic, that by refusing him she was 'as cruel as the sentence' he had passed on Claudio. Isabella turned away from him and sat huddled, her knees close to her chest, her eyes frightened.

For Isabella, this was a terrible failure, but Angelo interpreted her actions as part of a coy game, much like a child who withholds affection to manipulate her father. He slipped off the sofa to draw near, he put a friendly hand on her shoulder, then an arm, and pushed his face closer and closer, moving in for a kiss. Everything seemed to be set up for a romantic moment as if it were inevitable that Isabella would return the kiss. But she didn't. Repulsed, Angelo forced a suffocating kiss on to her lips and suddenly the tone of the scene turned from fumbling romantic comedy into violent sexual abuse. His sensual race given reign, Angelo threw Isabella onto the other sofa, apparently about to rape her, one hand holding her arm back, another stifling her face, the fire now bathing *his* face in a red glow that made him look demonic, and spelled out his bargain. Pulling her up again, Angelo pushed her to the floor outside his office and slammed the door behind her, leaving Isabella panting and miserable, prostrate, begging to no one, 'to whom should I complain?' (II.iv.172).

Thacker emphasized how alienated most of the characters were from their society, let down by both the ineffectual Duke and the oppressive Angelo. He added a number of shots to show how lonely most of the principals were: Marianna staring softly out of a window spattered with rain, the Duke rocking back and forth in front of a candle, Barnadine simpering with fear in his cell, Claudio feverish on his cell bed, the Provost quietly drinking in his office. Even Lucio became a melancholic drunk ruminating on the emptiness of his world and railing at those, the Duke and Pompey, who he saw as unable to see what he could see. Those characters that did not suit this *noir* mood were reduced or cut: Pompey's scenes were drastically thinned down, Elbow and Froth were both cut out altogether. In one scene, Thacker introduced an ironic twist for Pompey who was thrown into a cell with a feverish Claudio. Later, Pompey tenderly bathed Claudio's head. He was interrupted by the Provost, who came into the cell recruiting executioners. Pompey, the only person to give Claudio any comfort, got the job of beheading him. To underline the point, the Provost gave Claudio the order he had received for the execution. This was a world without consolation, and the loneliest scene of all was the very last one, with Isabella and the Duke staring each other in silence as the credits rolled.

Conclusion

Although both made by the BBC, Davis's and Thacker's films are totally contrasting: Davis deferred to the text, Thacker cut it up; Davis made a television studio look like a theatre, Thacker turned Shakespeare into a television writer; Davis tipped his hat to conventional performing styles, Thacker mixed medias. Yet, unexpectedly given these contrasts, Davis's and Thacker's interpretation of the play itself was not so different. In both, the Duke was insecure, his abrupt departure from office to wander the streets in disguise presented as a kind of mid-life crisis. Thacker's Isabella was a much more sexual and independent woman than Davis's mature, calm Isabella, yet Davis's Angelo was much sexier than Thacker's lecherous deputy. Of the two films, Thacker's is undoubtedly the more bold and arresting and made a statement not just about *Measure for Measure*, but about the best ways to transport Shakespeare into new media.

6 Critical Assessments

The Duke's sense of human responsibility is delightful throughout: he is a kindly father, and all the rest are his children. (Wilson Knight, p. 78)

Vincentio indeed is what Lucio calls him: 'the duke of dark corners,' addicted to disguises, sadistic teasings, and designs hopelessly duplicitous. (Bloom, p. 370)

A kindly father or a teasing sadist, a responsible human or a hopeless dupe? Harold Bloom and G. Wilson Knight's critical assessments seem so far apart that it is hard to imagine that they are writing about the same play. Would a reader who did not know that the Duke is also called Vincentio in the *dramatis personae* even realise that these two statements are about the same character? Here is Shakespeare's 'double-written' play exposed, two dukes appealing to two critical sensibilities, one so paternal he is almost touching divinity and may even *be* Christ, the other a cruel, obsessively nihilistic sexual sadist. It is worth pausing over these statements for a moment to reflect on how startling it is that they are so different. It is easy to blandly accept them as unremarkable instances of two different critics having different opinions (undergraduates might reasonably protest that they've never read two critics who shared the same opinion). But does anyone seriously argue that Lear is an understanding father, that Macbeth is a good host or that Falstaff is abstemious? How is *Measure for Measure* able to provoke such different and extreme interpretations of its main characters?

One reason is that the text itself, as written, lacks definitive statements about them. The Duke is a case in point. His reasons for leaving Vienna and returning in disguise are never satisfactorily established. Is he testing Angelo (and if so, why)? Or is he trying to engineer a grand finale of the kind that eventually happens in order to make a point about his authority? Harold Bloom calls the Duke 'weirdly motivated'; Harry Berger Jr agrees that he is 'weird' (Berger, p. 339). Shakespeare was nimble enough to write a play capable of addressing and challenging both court and city constituencies. In this regard, criticism faces the same challenge as performance: to find a way of binding the different elements of the play into a coherent whole and, in doing so, listen to the play's many silences and account for them. Isabella is not the only character who is quiet when we most want some lines from her: Barnadine and Claudio say nothing in their last scene, Angelo has no lines after his pardon, Juliet is quiet in all but one scene. Some critics see these ambiguities as the play's bottom line: 'the divergent assessments of the Duke result from significant omissions in the script', reassures Mary Ellen Lamb, who points out that the play 'is remarkable for the width of its gaps, for the absence of critical pieces of evidence which would enable us to choose one view or the other'. But *Measure for Measure* is not shoddily written. On the contrary, argues Lamb, it calls attention to theatre itself as an indeterminable, slippery art form and, through its gaps and silences, forces 'an ongoing flow of interpretations' (Lamb, p. 140).

It is tempting to leave *Measure for Measure* here as an intractably ambivalent play which can never be reconciled to either Wilson Knight's play about a kindly father or Bloom's play about a hopelessly duplicitous sadist. However, some critics are more daring and have proposed a range of ways to go beyond this position. In this chapter, I will explore some of the most important modern readings by approaching the play from two directions. First, I will look at critical interpretations which have sought in the text a 'grand design', a wider purpose which supplies a unity to the play not immediately evident on a superficial reading. Then I will look at readings which take as their starting point the play's representation of those who live on society's margins.

Grand designs

G. Wilson Knight was dazzled by *Measure for Measure's* extensive biblical allusions. Most critics now take the play's title as a political statement about the nature of justice, which is meted out 'measure for measure'. Wilson Knight latched on to its source in the Sermon on the Mount and begins his important essay with the relevant quote from St Matthew, 'Judge not, that ye be not judged.' This is not, in Wilson Knight's view, a political proposition but an ethical one and it is from this starting point that he reads *Measure for Measure* as an allegory of New Testament ethics. Each character represents an aspect of this allegory: Isabella is 'sainted purity', Angelo 'Pharisaical righteousness' and it is the Duke who is the Christ-figure, the centre point and moral focus of a 'psychologically sound and enlightened ethic' (Wilson Knight, pp. 73–4). The Duke has a secret plan which he outlines in Act I, scene iii and the rest of the play 'slowly unfolds the rich content of the Duke's plan' (p. 78). Peter Brook's 1950 production (discussed in Chapter 4) was of the play as Wilson Knight imagined it to be, and the notion that *Measure for Measure* is best understood as a religious allegory dominated critical responses for a generation. Before this, the general view was that the play was weakly constructed, its manifest narrative problems evidence of Shakespeare on a bad day. Coleridge had called it a 'hateful work' and many like him thought it 'unpleasant', even cynical. In 1942, L. C. Knights tried to account for his sense of discomfort about the play in an essay published in the journal *Scrutiny*. In the same issue, F. R. Leavis took Knights to task for his absurd misreading. He praised Wilson Knight and directly criticized productions which played the Duke as anything other than a Christ-figure: 'But then,' Leavis reflects, without irony, 'if you can't accept what Shakespeare does provide, you have, in some way, to import your interest and significance' (Leavis, p. 172).

The question of what Shakespeare – or, at least, the text – *does* provide is crucial to readings of the play. The Leavis–Wilson Knight position is now utterly redundant after a succession of critics have teased out the dark complexities of any treatment of religion in the Jacobean period – Shakespeare's use of Catholic imagery (from friars to nuns) is especially striking, given the intense religious divisions in his society. With hindsight, it looks like it is Leavis who is importing significance, but he is on the mark when he draws attention to (without quite seeing it himself) the imperative to supply a frame by which to understand the play. Wilson Knight was one of the first critics to try to rescue the play from a critical tradition which thought it problematic. He rejected the idea that *Measure for Measure* was a 'dark' comedy and found a unifying principle encoded in biblical references. Today, critics continue to look for a ruling idea, a 'grand design', to explain the play and many find this grand design in the Duke's plan. That is to say, if the Duke's scheme can be explained and accounted for, then the wider design of the play as a whole becomes clear. This runs the risk that critics end up seeing in the Duke's plans a reflection of their own critical preoccupations. No wonder, then, that the Duke is often seen as a cipher for Shakespeare himself: even Stephen Greenblatt is ready to see the Duke as 'an emblem of the playwright' (p. 138).

Contemporary criticism tends to look for Shakespeare/the Duke's grand design elsewhere than the Bible and one recurring trope is the 'Panopticon', a theoretical penal institution (designed by the nineteenth-century philosopher Jeremy Bentham) that enforces authority through surveillance rather than through stage-managed public displays of corporal punishment. This was discussed by Michel Foucault in his penal history *Discipline and Punish*, in which he used the Panopticon as a model for understanding how modern society regulates transgression. Although not in any sense about Shakespeare or *Measure for Measure*, Foucault's work inspired a new generation of critics who saw in *Measure for Measure* a powerful demonstration of this thesis in action. Important essays by Richard Wilson and Jonathan Goldberg established the terms of the debate. *Measure for Measure* is not about mercy and forgiveness, but about power and exploitation. The Duke's aim is not to teach his people a moral lesson, but to re-legitimate his rule first by reminding the city how bad things could be (if he acted like Angelo), then by appearing to magically restore power, when he has actually manipulated most characters. In effect, he 'scripts' the final scene, which is merely a public display of a knowledge which the Duke has only gained through covert, voyeuristic surveillance.

Taking his lead from Richard Wilson and Jonathan Goldberg, Kiernan Ryan, who calls the play a 'twisted, queasy comedy' (p. 133), develops a Foucauldian interest in power and exploitation. He goes further than Wilson by arguing that the play is a 'textbook' example of the transitional moment between medieval justice and the modern surveillance state, from 'a culture which asserts itself through spectacular, public displays of punitive violence' to 'one which secures subjection by subtler strategies of surveillance, concession and repressive tolerance' (p. 134). No wonder the play is queasy. Here, though, as Ryan himself points out, the Foucauldian reading is starting to look strained and unconvincing, a template which is being forced on to the text to the extent that, alarmingly, the play is literally turned on its head. *Measure for Measure*, surely, *ends* with a spectacular, public display: it *starts* with a strategy of surveillance. In the first scene, the Duke mutters that he does not like to 'stage me to their eyes' and shuffles off, hooded, to the prison to eavesdrop on his subjects. It is not they who get punished, it is those who exercise the Duke's power who end up being exposed (the Panopticon was never imagined to be a device to catch out the prison managers). The Duke actually fails to bring about a resolution through his disguised ruler game: if Angelo had pardoned Claudio, then the public display of Act V would have been unnecessary. The need for a punitive display follows the failure of a surveillance-based strategy to deliver justice; the Duke has to hastily improvise a new plan and he falls back on what was in fact a fairly conventional Renaissance display of justice and mercy. The fallacy is to suppose that the Duke all along intended to end the play thus: in truth, from the moment Angelo surprises him by not pardoning Claudio, when the bed-trick fails, the Duke is improvising, and one of the first things he does is to break cover with the Provost. His power to manipulate through disguise is running thin, hence his risky decision to include the Provost in his scheme.

The most convincing element of this reading is that several characters subject themselves to actions which appear to suit the state more than the individual. That is to say, they become 'willing agents of their own subjection' (p. 135). Angelo accepts his guilt and is not only ready to die, but also seems put out when the punishment is suspended. Isabella asks the Duke to show Angelo mercy, even though she still believes at this point that her brother is dead. On the face of it, these are indeed examples of the 'interpellation' of the subject by the state. The ideal subject for the modern state is one who polices itself, who does not need to be forced to do something because they are already convinced that what the state wants it to do is the right thing. This is the apex of ideological conquest – when the subject no longer realizes that they have been conquered. The Duke achieves this through the proto-modern political technology of voyeurism and Ryan, like many modern critics, finds it 'difficult not to see a prevision of the modern society in which power imposes itself not through force, but through the tyranny of transparency, by exposing everyone to the impersonal ubiquity of its remorseless gaze' (p. 135).

Does this notion stand up as a reading of *Measure for Measure*? To do so, the theory would have to show both events being produced by, and/or contingent upon, the Duke's surveillance strategy. Actually, both Angelo and Isabella are being consistent with the characters established for them in Act I and might just as well have come to this place in their character development without any involvement from the Duke – arguably, neither moves far from the character positions set out in the play's first scenes. Angelo has always been a stickler for the law and even says as much to Escalus in Act II, scene i: 'When I that censure him do so offend / Let mine own judgment pattern out my death' (ll. 29–30). He's as good as his word: so, when Angelo asks for death in Act V, scene i, he does so not because he has been indoctrinated or coerced, but because he has always believed in this medieval principle of justice (there is also a suggestion that, like Lucio, Angelo might feel that death is a more palatable punishment than marriage). In a curious way, Angelo's stance here is a resistance strategy: he does not, as Escalus does in Act II, scene i, accept the Duke's authority: 'Be it as your wisdom will', says Escalus, deferring to Angelo's better judgement; it is quite clear that Angelo thinks the Duke is wrong. By threatening death and showing mercy, the Duke might have at least hoped that Angelo would fall into line as a good interpellated subject. On the contrary, Angelo refuses to play ball and still entreats death after Isabella's remarkable speech.

Isabella is also being consistent with her character, in that she never thought Claudio had a strong case for clemency (she actually shows far more reluctance to plead for Claudio than she does for Angelo), and so can hardly complain that Angelo has executed the sentence which she herself called 'just'. However, Angelo did not commit the 'vice which most I do abhor' and should not be put to death for putting into practice the letter of the Duke's own law. If we put ourselves in Isabella's place, we might well find it difficult to forgive the man who had killed our brother – but then Isabella is not us, or even a real person. After all, this is the same Isabella who wanted Claudio's vice to 'meet the blow of justice', who resignedly gave up her brother for dead as early as Act II, scene ii when faced with Angelo's implacable legal logic: 'Oh just but severe law' (l. 42), she said, and her last words to Claudio in the play were ''Tis best that thou diest quickly' (III.i.150). Her rhetorical strategy in this final speech of hers is identical to the one she employed in her first pleas to Angelo. Her arguments then turned on separating the criminal from the crime: 'let it be his fault, / And not my brother' (II.ii.36–7) that is condemned to die. Her last words in the play read like one of the political slogans written during the student rebellion in Paris in 1968, with which Foucault was involved: 'Thoughts are no subjects / Intents but merely thoughts' (V.i.446–7). For Steven Mullaney, this is an ironic closure. He argues, with some force, that 'her plea for mercy is itself a manifest demonstration of the degree to which her thoughts have indeed become subjects, under the sway of a ruler who has adroitly if illicitly combined the power of secular and ghostly patriarchy' (p. 104). But how does the Duke influence her to make these arguments? He manipulates her in two ways: first, he does not reveal that he is the Friar (although by this point in the play that deception has been revealed), and so gains her confidence surreptitiously; second, he allows her to believe that Claudio is dead. Neither seems to point to a moment where Isabella forgives Angelo and so betrays the extent to which the state, via the Duke, has penetrated her thoughts and made them subjects. Isabella pleads for Angelo *despite* thinking that Claudio is dead. It is difficult to see how it is the Duke who is responsible for Isabella's speech. He does not provoke it; it is Marianna who pleads desperately to Isabella to kneel with her, and even she does not ask her to speak. Isabella does speak, however, and it is a dry speech which plainly and logically sets out the situation and comes to an inevitable conclusion.

Could it not be that Marianna and Isabella challenge the Duke here? Is this not another instance of the Duke's plan going wrong? Read this way, Isabella's last lines are tremendously affirmative, as is Marianna's part generally. Isabella has robbed the Duke of his best surprise. Presumably his plan had been to unveil Claudio and then pardon Angelo (which is what he does, as if sticking to the script that Isabella has tried to divert him from): Isabella's plea for Angelo is an unexpected and unplanned-for interruption which puts the Duke on the back foot by reminding him not only of Angelo's innocence, but Claudio's guilt. Isabella robs the Duke of the sovereign's privilege of conveying mercy to his subjects. This speech is hardly in the same submissive league as Kate's homily to marriage at the end of *The Taming of the Shrew*: Isabella's is a dissonant, even dissident, intervention that directly challenges not just the Duke's sentence, but the logic of justice which underlies it.

In reading the significance of Isabella's plea, Wilson Knight and Ryan, though applying apparently different critical paradigms, make the same basic assumption: that making Isabella (believe she chooses to) forgive Angelo is part of the Duke's grand design. In Wilson Knight's Christian reading, her choice illustrates the ethics of free will and Christian morality; in Ryan's reading (and Mullaney's), her choice is the product of a false consciousness imprinted by power. All three take for granted that the Duke has 'adroitly' scripted events, when Shakespeare quite plainly shows the Duke inventing plots on the hoof in Act IV when his real grand design, to 'save the day' without ever revealing his authority, falls apart. How on earth would the Duke have got to this place if the bed-trick had worked? For me, the most worrying aspect of this argument is that Isabella is reduced to nothing more than a ventriloquist dummy. This is an area where performance runs ahead of critical thinking. For example, take this brilliant insight from Juliet Stevenson, who played the part in 1983:

> The last character to be put on trial is the Duke. Having meted out all those judgments, he turns round, and there's Lucio! Lucio, who's slandered him, abused him, dogged him with calumny. And the Duke says, 'Hang him!'
>
> As Isabella, I stood and looked at him. Watching to see what he would do. Because unless the Duke takes on the trial of *himself*, which involves

bringing himself to let Lucio off the hook, to exercise forgiveness, he hasn't learned the capacity for mercy from Isabella . . . He watched me watching, turned back to Lucio, and reprieved the death sentence. (Rutter, p. 52)

Note here that it is *Isabella* who becomes the voyeur, the panoptic guard: it is she who watches the Duke, the Duke who capitulates under the female gaze. Another actress, Paola Dionisotti, admitted that 'What I never got in the role was her final strength' (p. 39); Stevenson calls her 'the most courageous character in the play' (p. 26). To see Isabella, at the end, as an interpellated subject, not only vastly overstates the Duke's plans (which read to me more like a series of mishaps than an artful political/moral design), but also reduces Isabella to an ideological automaton.

These readings depend in part on a wilful misreading of Foucault's thesis as well as *Measure for Measure*. Foucault firmly situates the emergence of the surveillance state to the end of the eighteenth century, that period when public executions rapidly declined and punishment was subjected to the logic of the ledger book: that is to say, nearly two centuries after Shakespeare's death. So ubiquitous is the Panopticon in modern discussion of the play that it is sobering to remember first that the Panopticon was a nineteenth-century design (and consequently to apply it backwards to the seventeenth century is absurdly ahistorical) and secondly, was never, and has never, been built. Foucault uses Bentham's Panopticon to illustrate a paradigm shift in the conception of punishment: to apply this fictive thought-experiment backwards to read *Measure for Measure* is highly problematic and misses the sense of humour in both Shakespeare *and* Foucault. If there is anything incipiently modern about the play, it is that it shows the shortcomings of power-by-surveillance and, although it does so by falling back on a medieval justice system that is almost as imperfect, there is enough in the play to allow modern performances to think about the different ways in which power is practised now.

These ideas are part of the New Historicism which emerged in the late 1980s as a challenge to orthodox ways of locating texts in history. The nub of New Historicist *Measure for Measure*s is that the Duke's political rule and the ideology which supports it are in practice affirmed by the Duke's activities in the final scene. This is the subtle position best articulated by Stephen Greenblatt, who argues that the play presents a model of a political structure which depends for its survival on a limited form of licensed subversion. That is to say, any deviance or challenge to authority is only there because it is permitted. This is what distinguishes Angelo's rigidly authoritarian rule from the Duke's more lax regime. Angelo brooks no exceptions and enforces the letter of the law absolutely, and he fails. The Duke, on the other hand, recognizes when it is right to enforce a law, when it is right to show mercy, and so on. Comedy as licensed subversion is a tradition that arguably derives from folk festivals such as the Lord of Misrule, where the servants become the masters for a day. The point of such festivals is to demonstrate why it is important and 'natural' for the accepted authority to rule as it does. Greenblatt takes a complex view of *Measure for Measure*: the resolution reaffirms the Duke's authority and the subversive forces represented by Lucio, Pompey, etc., are contained, his rule renewed, albeit with 'ironic reservations' (Greenblatt, p. 29). This is a perceptive reading, but leaves us again with a 'grand design' to demonstrate a moral principle of power and, as we have seen, it is in practice difficult to find evidence in the text to support the notion of the Duke's grand design. We risk believing the Duke's theatrical bluff that everything has been planned, but very little of what happens in Act V seems to go according to plan. Dawson makes a similar point in his cogent critique of the New Historicist position. He argues that the final scene is made up of three climaxes, each one an unveiling: Marianna reveals her identity, the Friar becomes the Duke, and Claudio is unmuffled. Each one promises 'closure' but ends up deferring it, which Dawson reads as an 'over-compensation' on the Duke's part: 'Theatrical power, unsure of itself, trips itself up . . . it is the theatrical itself which is being called into question; the theatrical as a mode of generic manipulation' (Dawson, p. 338). Far from reigning subversion in, the execution of power through theatre (read as licensed subversion) produces subversive effects: the end is, Dawson argues, 'self-subverting'. The subversion-containment reading also rests on a contentious view of the play, that its chief concern is the regulation of (mainly sexual) subversion. The Duke's work in the denouement is not directed at Mistress Overdone or Pompey or even really at Lucio (who is dragged in for quite different reasons); it is directed at Angelo. What is to be contained is not the wild suburbs of London, but Angelo's over-anxious authoritarianism. The only subversive to be contained is Angelo and, possibly, Isabella: Barnadine, however, escapes. Pompey does not run riot in the play, Angelo does.

On the margins

Is there any character in Shakespeare with fewer lines than Barnadine who attracts as much devotion? 'Sublime Barnadine', raptures Bloom, who marvels at the recalcitrant death-rower's 'wisdom to stay perpetually drunk because to be sober in this mad play is to be madder than the maddest' (Bloom, p. 359). Barnadine is a 'genius of that disorder' and so qualifies as the play's 'imaginative centre (and greatest glory)'. In surveying the play's last act, Bloom equates Isabella's silence with Barnadine's: 'Nothing is more meaningful in this scene', he insists, 'than the total silence of Barnadine.' Bloom thinks the play nihilistic: 'all that remains is the marvellous image of the dissolute murderer Barnadine, who gives us a minimal hope for the human as against the state, by being unwilling to die for any man's persuasion' (p. 380). Barnadine is the prisoner whose execution is brought forward so that the Provost can have a severed head with which to fool Angelo. Jonathan Dollimore thinks that Barnadine's 'careless refusal of subjection' is one of the play's most subversive moments (Dollimore, p. 83). Jacques Lezra marvels at what he calls Barnadine's Pirandellian refusal which 'marks him from the first as a figure designating the limits of the Duke's power' (Lezra, p. 255). Barnadine refuses to participate in the play and he 'brings to the play a desperate mortality marked by an equally profound and roiling undecidability' (p. 272). Bernthal agrees that he is the play's 'most subversive role' (p. 262). Barnadine has only seven lines.

Modern critics are often more interested in the play's marginal characters than they are in any of the principals. Pompey Bum, Mistress Overdone, Lucio, Elbow, Froth and Juliet represent a richly dramatized class who live on the edges of the Duke's authority. If the Duke does have a grand design, it is related in some way to these people and it is tempting to see in them reflections of the play's first London audiences. It is they whose lax sexual morality provokes Angelo's strict rules, but they also have a victory of sorts as Angelo ends up hoist by his own petard. Even absent characters have attracted critical attention, as in Jacques Lezra's fascinating essay on Ragazine, the pirate whose sole appearance is in Act IV, scene iii as a severed head and who is, argues Lezra, a 'peculiarly over-determined, over-convenient sign' (Lezra, p. 265) that enables Barnadine's subversion *and* facilitates the Duke's new master-plot. Lezra's witty essay shows how deep the connections are between the play and the language of piracy, with the head acting as a sort of a cipher. Dollimore centres his reading of the play on 'absent characters' and 'the history which it [the play] contains yet does not represent' (Dollimore, p. 73). The absentees, it turns out, are the prostitutes who are the object of Angelo's crackdown.

Dollimore begins his essay by outlining two contrasting positions on the characters he calls, as most do (but not for any clear reason), the 'low-lifes'. One follows on from the discussion about 'grand designs' in the last section: 'unrestrained sexuality,' he writes, 'is ostensibly subverting social order; anarchy threatens to engulf the State unless sexuality is subjected to renewed and severe regulation'. The play is, then, a meditation on how best to deal with sexual anarchy, the Duke's surveillance strategy versus Angelo's outright oppression. Weighing up this position, with which he disagrees, Dollimore is surprised that critics so readily see sexual transgression in the play in the same terms that Angelo does, that is to say as a threat to order. Angelo, after all, is the least reliable moral critic of them all. The obvious counter-reading would be to celebrate Shakespeare's representation of sexual transgression and talk about it in terms of a liberal force that authorities need to contain because they are themselves sexually repressed. Dollimore dismisses such a reading as 'scarcely less appropriate', for it does little more than reverse the terms of the first argument. To accept either position would be to engage in a long argument about which 'side' is good and which bad: the idealistic ruler vs the sexual sinner, the priggish judge vs the 'happy whore'? Dollimore is right: none of these oppositions will do (p. 73).

This is where absent characters become important: 'Whatever subversive identity the sexual offenders in this play possess is a construction put upon them by the authority which wants to control them.' In other words, a prostitute and a lecher are identities imposed from above. Dollimore continues: 'moreover control is exercised through that construction'. It is only when 'diverse and only loosely associated sexual offenders' are identified as a 'category of offender' that they acquire the capacity to be (or rather, to be thought of as) dangerous; they are 'demonised as a threat to the law'. A cursory glance at any red-top tabloid newspaper is likely to yield many examples of social panic about certain kinds of people in our society which is out of proportion to the actual threat posed. Dollimore points out that though Angelo may fret about the consequences of moral laxity, the play itself shows the transgressors themselves entirely incapable of any kind of organized subversion:

> the play discloses corruption to be an effect less of desire than of author-ity itself. It also shows how corruption is downwardly identified – that is, focused and placed with reference to low-life 'licence'; in effect, and espe-cially in the figure of Angelo, corruption is displaced from authority *to* desire and by implication from the rulers to the ruled. (p. 73)

In short, it suits those in power to blame others to distract from their own shortcomings. The period was full of proclamations which frothed about 'dissolute and dangerous persons'. One was of imme-diate relevance to Shakespeare: in 1603, the year before he wrote *Measure for Measure*, a proclamation was issued to tear down some houses in London. This was a pragmatic attempt to control the plague, but it also included unnecessary swipes at 'excessive numbers of idle, indigent, dissolute and dangerous persons' (p. 77). These people were easy targets and proclamations like this painted a picture of sub-urban life in London's liberties which was out of all proportion to what actually went on in them. Shakespeare may refer directly to it in Act I, scene ii, when Pompey, Lucio and Mistress Overdone discuss Angelo's proclamation that houses of ill-repute are to be torn down (the same scene contains several references to disease as well). In Dollimore's reading, these people are only 'low-lifes' and marginal in the discourse of an authority which needs to constantly reaffirm itself by defining invisible threats and ungovernable menaces threatening stability and order. Shakespeare neither condemns the prostitutes, but nor does he celebrate them. Rather, he gives those demonized by authority a voice, even if that voice does more to reveal such strategies than it does to challenge them. This is a justly celebrated essay, pivotal for critical assessments of the play. It is not without its shortcomings: as Lisa Hopkins points out, Dollimore's treatment of Isabella as a coerced and subordinated character ignores the interpretative possibilities that her (perhaps radical?) silence opens up (Hopkins, pp. 96–7).

There are other ways of addressing the critical impasse that Dollimore identified at the start of the essay, and most focus in some way on sexuality. Mary Thomas Crane, for example, writes that *Measure for Measure* 'is largely about the terrifying permeability of the human body and the embodied brain and thus about the internal properties that made the early modern self both vulnerable and resistant to the workings of disciplinary power' (Crane, p. 275). Carolyn Brown has little doubt that the most disturbing sexual transgressors are in fact the Duke and Isabella. As Janet Adelman first noted, the Duke is a voyeur; he looks but he does not touch. Brown develops this point by noting the odd eroticism of some of Isabella's lines which, when quoted out of context, suddenly seem much kinkier than you might expect: 'Th'impression of keen whips I'd wear as rubies / And strip myself to death' (II.iv.101–2). The Duke and Isabella get their kicks by getting other people to have sex for them (i.e. Marianna and Angelo) and then describing it to each other: 'They both aspire to live saintly existences, professing to be the epitome of morality and chastity, and yet they engage in what often seem to be unethical, sexually charged acts' (Brown, pp. 190–1).

Measure for Measure attracts such provocative readings. So much of it is about politics, death/disease and sexual transgression, all of which are interrelated, sometimes in unexpected ways. With so many gaps and silences to account for, critics are able to adopt with conviction a number of different critical positions, some wildly inventive. *Measure for Measure* is a Christian allegory, a political fable, a nihilistic fantasy, a voice for the repressed, an index of social tensions, a crazy 'S&M' romp. Modern criticism has moved decisively away from what was once a dominant tradition of Christian-based interpretation. Instead, the terms of most contemporary criticism are political and sexual: the exercise of authority, the relationship between power and punishment, the question about *who* is deviant, and the most crucial modern question of all (one which usually separates critics), what is and what *isn't* resolved by the play's conclusion?

Further Reading

I have used Brian Gibbon's edition of *Measure for Measure* throughout (Cambridge: Cambridge University Press, 1991).

I   The text and performance

N. W. Bawcutt (ed.), *Measure for Measure*, Oxford World Classics (Oxford: Oxford University Press, 1998).

British Universities Film and Video Council, http://www.bufvc.ac.uk.

Peter Brook, *The Empty Space* (London: MacGibbon & Kee, 1968).

Penny Gay, *As She Likes It: Shakespeare's Unruly Women* (London: Routledge, 1994).

Gareth Lloyd-Evans, 'Directing Problem Plays: John Barton talks to Gareth Lloyd-Evans', *Shakespeare Survey*, 25 (Cambridge: Cambridge University Press, 1972), pp. 63–72.

S. Nagarajan, '*Measure for Measure on Stage and Screen*', in S. Nagarajan (ed.), *Measure for Measure*. Signet Classic. 3rd edn (Harmondsworth: Penguin, 1998), pp. 180–212.

Graham Nicholls, *Measure for Measure – Text and Performance* (London: Macmillan, 1986).

Edward L. Rocklin, 'Measured Endings: How Productions from 1720 to 1929 Close Shakespeare's Open Silences in *Measure for Measure*', *Shakespeare Survey*, 53 (Cambridge: Cambridge University Press, 2000), pp. 213–232.

Lawrence J. Ross, *On Measure for Measure: An Essay in Criticism of Shakespeare's Drama* (Newark: University of Delaware Press, 1997).

Royal Shakespeare Company, www.rsc.org.uk.

Carol Chillington Rutter, *Clamorous Voices: Shakespeare's Women Today* (London: The Women's Press, 1988).

Michael Scott, *Renaissance Drama and a Modern Audience* (London: Macmillan, 1982).

Robert Speaight, *Shakespeare on the Stage* (London: Collins, 1973).

Peter Thomson, 'The Royal Shakespeare Season 1970 Reviewed', *Shakespeare Survey*, 24 (Cambridge: Cambridge University Press, 1971), pp. 63–73.

Alice Venezky, 'The 1950 Season at Stratford-upon-Avon – A Memorable Achievement in Stage History', *Shakespeare Quarterly*, 2:1 (1951), pp. 73–7.

Herbert S. Weil, 'The Options of the Audience: Theory and Practice in Peter Brook's *Measure for Measure*', *Shakespeare Survey*, 25 (Cambridge: Cambridge University Press, 1972), pp. 27–35.

Susan Willis, *The BBC Shakespeare Plays: Making the Televised Canon* (Chapel Hill and London: University of North Carolina Press, 1991).

II   Genre and problem plays

Harry Berger, Jnr., *Making Trifles of Terrors: Redistributing Complicities in Shakespeare* (Chicago: Stanford University Press, 1997).

Lisa Hopkins, *Beginning Shakespeare* (Manchester: Manchester University Press, 2005).

Jean E. Howard, '*Measure for Measure* and the Restraints of Convention', *Essays in Literature*, 10:2 (Fall 1983), pp. 149–58.

G. Wilson Knight, *The Wheel of Fire: Interpretations of Shakespearean Tragedy*, 2nd edn (London: Methuen, 1949).

L. C. Knights, 'Ambiguity in *Measure for Measure*', *Scrutiny*, X (1942), 2:25.

F. R. Leavis, *The Common Pursuit* (London: Chatto and Windus, 1952).

Alexander Leggatt, 'Substitution in *Measure for Measure*', *Shakespeare Quarterly*, 39 (1988), pp. 342–59.

Leah Marcus, *Puzzling Shakespeare: Local Readings and its Discontents* (Los Angeles: University of California Press, 1988).

III   Gender and sexuality

Janet Adelman, *Suffocating Mothers: Fantasies of Maternal Origin in Shakespeare's Plays* (London and New York: Routledge, 1992).

Carolyn E. Brown, 'Erotic Religious Flagellation and Shakespeare's *Measure for Measure*', *English Literary Renaissance*, 16 (1988), pp. 139–65.

—— 'The Wooing of Duke Vincentio and Isabella of *Measure for Measure*: "The Image of it Gives [them] Content" ', *Shakespeare Studies*, 22 (1994), pp. 189–219.

Mary Thomas Crane, 'Male Pregnancy and Cognitive Permeability in *Measure for Measure*', *Shakespeare Quarterly*, 49:3 (Autumn 1998), pp. 269–92.

Marc Shell, *The End of Kinship*: Measure for Measure, *Incest and the Ideal of Universal Siblinghood* (Chicago: Stanford University Press, 1988).

IV   Cultural contexts and politics

Craig A. Bernthal, 'Staging Justice: James I and the Trial Scenes of *Measure for Measure*.' *Studies in English Literature*, 32 (1992), pp. 247–69.

Harold Bloom, *Shakespeare: The Invention of the Human* (New York: Riverhead, 1998).

Anthony B. Dawson, '*Measure for Measure*, New Historicism, and Theatrical Power', *Shakespeare Quarterly*, 39:3 (Autumn 1988), pp. 328–41.

Jonathan Dollimore, 'Transgression and Surveillance in *Measure for Measure*', in Jonathan Dollimore and Alan Sinfield, eds., *Political Shakespeare: New Essays in Cultural Materialism*, 2nd edn (Manchester: Manchester University Press, 1994), pp. 72–87.

Michel Foucault, *Discipline and Punish: The Birth of the Prison*, trans. Alan Sheridan (Harmondsworth: Penguin, 1977).

Jonathan Goldberg, *James I and the Politics of Literature: Jonson, Shakespeare, Donne and their Contemporaries* (Baltimore and London: Johns Hopkins University Press, 1983).

Stephen Greenblatt, *Shakespearean Negotiations: The Circulation of Social Energy in Renaissance England* (Oxford: Clarendon Press, 1988).

Elizabeth Hanson, *Discovering the Subject in Renaissance England* (Cambridge: Cambridge University Press, 1998).

A. V. Judges (ed.), *The Elizabethan Underworld* (London: Routledge, 1930).

Mary Ellen Lamb, 'Shakespeare's "Theatrics": Ambivalence toward Theatre in *Measure for Measure*', *Shakespeare Studies*, 20 (1987), pp. 129–46.

Jacques Lezra, 'Pirating Reading: The Appearance of History in *Measure for Measure*', *English Literary History*, 56:2 (Summer 1989), pp. 255–92.

Russ McDonald (ed.), *The Bedford Companion to Shakespeare: An Introduction with Documents*, 2nd edn (Boston and New York: Bedford/St.Martin's, 2001).

Steven Mullaney, *The Place of the Stage: License, Play, and Power in Renaissance England* (Ann Arbor: University of Michigan Press, 1988).

Tanya Pollard (ed.), *Shakespeare's Theatre: A Sourcebook* (Oxford: Blackwell, 2004).

Kiernan Ryan, *Shakespeare*, 3rd edn (Basingstoke: Palgrave, 2002).

J. B. Steane (ed.), *Thomas Nashe: The Unfortunate Traveller and Other Works* (Harmondsworth: Penguin, 1971).

Leonard Tennenhouse, *Power on Display: The Politics of Shakespeare's Genres* (London: Methuen, 1988).

Richard Wilson, *Will Power: Essays on Shakespearean Authority* (Hemel Hempstead: Harvester Wheatsheaf, 1993).

Nigel Wood (ed.), *Measure for Measure* (Buckingham and Philadelphia: Open University Press, 1996).

Index